RICHARD BY KATHRYN

RICHARD BY KATHRYN
The Life of Richard Whiteley

Kathryn Apanowicz

Foreword by Carol Vorderman

First published in Great Britain in 2006 by
Virgin Books Ltd
Thames Wharf Studios
Rainville Road
London
W6 9HA

A catalogue record for this book is available from
the British Library.

ISBN (10) 1 8522 7375 5
ISBN (13) 978 1 8522 7375 5

The paper used in this book is a natural, recyclable product
made from wood grown in sustainable forests. The
manufacturing process conforms to the regulations of the
country of origin.

Typeset by TW Typesetting, Plymouth, Devon
Printed and bound in Great Britain by
Mackays of Chatham PLC

CONTENTS

To dearest Dick
and all those who made him smile.

FOREWORD
By Carol Vorderman

I first met Kathy nearly twenty years ago. I'd gone into Richard's dressing room on *Countdown* to have a cup of tea and she was in there, perched on a table making him laugh. Theirs was a relationship which would grow into a deep love, once Richard found it in him to settle.

I haven't told this publicly before, but about six months before he died, Richard told me that he was going to marry Kathy.

He and I would often joke about how we were allergic to marriage – he'd been divorced once, and I twice. He would banter on *Countdown* about how 'I'd been to all of Carol's weddings'. I would challenge him on how many fondue sets he still had locked in his attic (they were a popular but useless wedding present in the 70s when he had been married). Mention the word marriage to Richard and he would turn pale. He told me he would even switch off his mobile phone on 29 February every leap year (the day women are traditionally allowed to pop the question) so that no-one could get hold of him, just in case. And then the year before he died, he'd realised just how much Kathy meant to him.

When we were on our way to the studio I'd said something about weddings 'ha ha ha' and he turned to me, with a solemn expression, and said 'I'm going to marry her'. 'Ha ha ha' I said again, and he said 'No, I mean it. We're going to get married. I know how much she means to me and how stupid I've been.'

Later at lunch I said to him, 'Are you serious about that?' 'Oh yes, I'm serious,' he replied. I asked him about it many times as I was teasing him that I couldn't be left as the only unmarried one. But he was serious and I was delighted for him. In his typical way, he was working up to asking Kathy herself. He hadn't done it.

As we all know now, Richard became ill before he could carry out his wish.

Over the years they had been together, Kathy had made Richard laugh more than anyone. I had a theory about Richard and bossy women. He seemed to love having bossy women around him. His sister Helen (who was one of the most charming women you could ever meet) was always telling him off. Kathy often had to keep him in check. I was forever tut-tutting in his direction. Christa Ackroyd (who presented *Calendar* with him every night for 12 years) is a formidable woman. Somehow, by having all of us around in different parts of his life, he could remain a little boy at heart because we were all watching out for him (to many different degrees I admit) and in our own ways, we all adored him – and the little monkey knew it.

In August 2001, Kathy and Richard and my partner Des Kelly and I had been invited to Prince Charles's Highgrove Estate to a formal dinner where HRH and Camilla Parker Bowles (as she then was) were to be in attendance. It was a beautiful evening. But then we switched on the news as we were getting ready and the lead item said 'Bong . . . Prince Charles rushed to hospital after falling from horse.' He'd been playing polo and fallen from his pony and was temporarily unconscious. Obviously he couldn't come to the dinner, so he sent Princes William and Harry instead. Two Princes for the price of one. What a bargain! We wandered around the stunning gardens and then plonked ourselves on our tables. The invitations said that carriages were strictly at 11 p.m. and we were obviously going to behave. Now the four of us along with David Jason and his wife Gill (who'd previously worked on *Countdown* in the early days) were on a lovely table with Camilla. We had a wonderful time, but the gentleman who was serving wine to our table was a real *Countdown*er. He had watched for nearly 20 years and never missed a show. As our reward, he kept plying us with extra bottles of champagne, wine and anything we wanted. In the end, David Jason was doing Del Boy impressions for us, Whiters was serving drinks and I was just curled up laughing. What a night! The six of us were the last to leave at about 2 a.m. The taxi had gone home without us and I can't even remember how we got back to our bed and breakfast. Then Kathy started singing songs from the musicals (which Whiters always loved) and it was hard to get up in the morning. Richard had that way about him. He'd break rules in the nicest way, never a bad boy, just mischievous.

Richard Whiteley was a special man. He was full of contradictions but in his soul he only ever wanted to laugh and be loved and he always, always wanted the best for people. He loved to gossip but wasn't a troublemaker. He would get irritable but hated arguments. He worked hard all his life but he always believed he was lucky. In this tricky world of television, there are many egos but he loved his to be popped on a regular basis. His pomposity would come and go, but it only ever lasted for a few minutes until he'd burst out laughing with the ridiculousness of it all. He adored parties and in many ways, he was a party within himself. Wherever he was, there would be fun. He hated to be alone and yet he liked peaceful places.

I never saw Richard in hospital. I sent him cards and trinkets and I hope he knew how much I loved him. I believe he was far more important in my life than I ever was in his but that didn't matter. It was a joy to know him and a privilege to have been so close to him.

Richard died the day before we were due to record the first ever *Countdown*s without him in the chair. We were getting a series of guest presenters to present a week of *Countdown* each, just until he was well enough to come back. Those shows were never made.

Richard recorded his last *Countdown* in April 2005. It was the final of Series 53. We had made just under 4,000 programmes together over 23 years. He opened the show by saying 'Welcome to the final *Countdown*.' It was his play on words, but he'd never said it before and so I glared at him across the studio and told him I didn't like him saying that. He laughed, as usual, and pretended to correct himself 'I mean welcome to the final of *Countdown*.'

Whenever a conundrum is revealed on *Countdown*, the letters are jumbled up so that contestants have to unjumble them to guess the nine-letter word. Richard's final conundrum on his last-ever *Countdown* was the nine-letter word FALSI-FIED. When he revealed it, the letters were arranged as LIFE FAIDS.

Maybe it's easy to look back on these things and think they are somehow prophetic. Maybe it is merely coincidence. Maybe if we'd never made that show he'd still be here.

I'm glad that Kathy has put this book together. It's just a shame it ever had to be.

PREFACE

In 2000 Richard wrote a memoir, a good-humoured third party look at aspects of his work. He didn't want to reveal anything of himself – at the time it was too soon. No mention of his many friends, male and female. And he was not yet emotionally ready to deal with the tragic deaths in his family.

He had always intended a sequel – he says so at the end of the book – and left me all the papers to write one, as well as thousands of private photographs.

I wasn't around for all of his life, certainly not the first 16 years – I wasn't born – so I have spoken to many of his friends and colleagues for their memories of him. Richard was not a man to let go of his past and most of his chums came through The Parsonage, where we lived, at one time or other. It became clear, as we talked, that they remembered their times with him with laughter and affection. As I do. He was a true friend to those who knew him personally and, through television, also a friend for millions of those who didn't. He was also the man I loved. This book is our tribute to him.

ONE

To begin at the end, Richard died on Sunday, 26 June 2005. He was only 61. The last year of his life had been one of the best. Twelve months previously, almost to the day, a dream of his had been realised: two vowels and a consonant. He was a stout believer in all things British and he revered the Honours system, hoping one day that he might be recognised. The fact that he was recognised nearly everywhere, anyway, without the need for a gong seemed almost to be lost on him.

He had accepted his OBE in advance, of course, by post but he was concerned that the public announcement of it should come as a surprise to me. There is a Palace embargo on the news until Saturday morning so the first to break it tend to be the radio stations at 12.00 midnight on that day. Richard had carefully planned that we would be driving home from the Timeform dinner at York Racecourse and he would casually turn on Radio Five and I would be bowled over by the news, maybe annoyed that he had kept it secret.

At the time I was hosting an afternoon show on Radio York. The Friday before, Richard, a forty-year veteran of presenting news television, remembered that the Honours Lists went out to the media the day before so they could do their interviews. So he rang the manager at the radio station and asked that on no account should I be allowed to see it.

Unfortunately somebody had earlier come down from the newsroom and casually mentioned to me: 'You'll need a hat, then?'

I didn't follow her.

'You'll need a hat,' she repeated, 'to go to the Palace.'

'What are you talking about?'

'Richard's in the Honours List. He's got an OBE.'

He was at York Races and his mobile phone was off but I called and left a message saying: 'I know – and I intend to buy a very expensive hat.'

An OBE may not seem a big deal to some people – Melvyn Bragg is a lord and lots of actors have been knighted – but to Richard it meant everything. It was a vindication of his career – 'for services to broadcasting'. A broadcaster: that is all he had ever wanted to be since his dad photographed him at the age of eight outside the BBC. In fact he worked for Yorkshire Television – 25 years as the face of Yorkshire on *Calendar*, and 23, slightly overlapping, years on *Countdown*.

He was a broadcaster and whether you're on hospital radio or national TV or international satellite, you still try to communicate as best you can. With Richard, in the past year or two, he had, unwittingly, communicated himself into cult status. The strange way he had entered into so many people's lives was something that nobody fully realised until after his death.

We duly went to dinner at York after the races. On the drive back to our home, in the Dales, he switched to BBC's Radio Five and news of his OBE was among the Honours they chose to report. There were three people in the studio to review the papers and one, presumably brought in for her strong opinions, thought that it was 'absurd to honour people like Richard Whiteley. All he does is sit around in those silly jumpers.' Clearly she had got him confused with Gyles Brandreth. But research was not her strong suit.

You silly bloody woman, I thought, you don't know what he's done. This man, whenever he is asked, will draw the raffle in the tiniest village hall. He has given so much time to people. He was always helpful. The number of people I've met in television who said: 'I wrote to him when I was at school or university and he invited me to come and see YTV (Yorkshire Television).'

Dick (as I usually called him) carefully chose one of the dates when the Queen would be presenting the Honours. I went with his niece Georgie and his son James. When the Queen asked him what sort of broadcasting he did, he dutifully replied 'Daytime. I do a show called *Countdown*.' She gave him a knowing smile. She watched it after Channel 4 racing; he knew because her sister had told him.

Friends from Yorkshire and London joined us for a slap-up lunch at the Ritz afterwards. Carol Vorderman buzzed around excitedly, snapping every moment – something that amused the Barclay twins, owners of the hotel, who were sitting at the next table.

For just one moment I caught a wistful look on Richard's face and asked him what was wrong. Of course, three of the people who had mattered most to him were not with us to celebrate. Seven years previously his sister, Helen, had died of liver cancer. She was 48. That was followed by the death of his mother, Margaret, and then, at the age of only 28, Helen and her husband James's daughter, Alex, died of cystic fibrosis. There seemed to be a tragic curse on Richard's family.

After pudding, when he hoped the distinguished dining room had cleared, Richard had arranged for CJ, a girl who had appeared in one of Gyles Brandreth's shows, to lead us in a sing-song around the Ritz grand piano. It was marvellous. We sang Gershwin and show tunes and Frank Sinatra and Richard's favourites like 'I've Got Rhythm' and '76 Trombones', anything big and rousing. That was the way we tended to end the evening when people came for a meal. Once we went on a friend's yacht and just sang for a week.

It was his favourite thing: to have a bloody good lunch and a big sing-song. He loved 'One for my Baby': 'It's quarter to three. There's no-one in the place. 'Cept you and me. So set 'em up, Joe.' I think he rather romantically thought that he was sitting in a bar on his own with a drink in his hand. Because he always was the very last to leave, a fact that often used to drive me nuts.

He just couldn't bear to miss anything. Some nights we would be dashing about to three parties. I would suggest that it might be nice if we could go to just one of them. 'But I promised,' he would plead. I think he thought that there might be somebody having a better time than he was.

He did his *Countdown*s during the week and at the weekends we would often go to the races – he had shares in three horses – Al Ava Consonant which was not a huge success, Mare of Wetwang which did win a couple of times, and Twice Nightly which didn't win oncely.

The autumn of 2004 was peaceful, with winter slow to come. We took long walks, which always included a pub, a fire and usually some local friends.

Richard adored the North Riding and even wrote a column about it in *Dales Life* – although this tended to be less about the flora and fauna and more about parking restrictions in Middleham or new one-way systems in Leyburn. He didn't like change.

At Christmas we went, as usual, to Giggleswick School for the carol service. The candlelit chapel and the treble singing 'Once in Royal David's City' sent shivers down the spine. For him it brought back the carefree days of his childhood. More than that, it was very much part of English tradition, something he clung to like a vice.

We spent Christmas Eve of 2004 at The Parsonage. It was a lean gathering, just James, the late Helen's husband, who had become a judge, and his surviving daughter, Georgina – not the huge family gathering of days of yore, but it was surprisingly enjoyable, warm and happy. They stayed the night and the next morning we were like children, thrilled as we unwrapped presents. Dick gave me a huge box. I groaned silently at Georgie, fearing it might be a computer – the last thing I wanted to do was set up a computer on Christmas Day. But it was a sleek flat-screen television, which I treasured.

We escaped to Birmingham for Christmas Day to stay with Richard's former co-presenter Bob Warman, his wife Di, and their children Guy and Claudia. Bob made the move back from Leeds to the Midlands twenty years ago and has remained the 6.00 p.m. rock of the local news, a famous and trusted face.

He was the only person to call Richard 'Ricco'. They relaxed in each other's company and liked to go on holiday together. After lunch, Bob told the family about their first one which was to Malta in 1979. Richard was well known in Yorkshire through *Calendar* and Bob was doing his first stint presenting *ATV Today* in the Midlands. They decided to go to a restaurant in Sliema which was popular with British tourists. Richard, who loved playing games, suggested to Bob that the first of them to be recognised would be treated to dinner by the other.

Bob agreed. They walked into the restaurant and the Maltese barman immediately said in a thick accent: 'Bob Warman. *ATV Today*.'

Richard was incredulous and not a little miffed that a native of Malta should cause him to lose the bet. He asked the barman how he knew Bob and the chap confessed he had done time in Leicester Jail and the telly was on every night in the recreation room.

'Sorry, Ricco,' said Bob, 'but you're paying.'

'It doesn't count,' Richard replied, turning to the barman. 'You didn't *choose* to watch him.'

The Warman children broke up in laughter.

The days after Boxing Day were always ones that Richard could happily have abolished like Alan Rickman's order to 'Cancel Christmas' in *Robin Hood, Prince of Thieves*.

His birthday fell on 28 December and then there was New Year's Eve, grim reminders to him of the passing of time and the inevitability of change. It wasn't that Richard thought he was Peter Pan and didn't want to grow up. It was just that he was 61, retired from Yorkshire Television, and, although he did not want for money, he had few hobbies that would fill his later years: no fishing or golf or DIY or gardening. He loved the here and now, not just *Countdown* but its spin-offs, meeting new people, doing guest shots, opening things, closing the bar.

James, his 17-year-old son, came up for a couple of days and we went for lunch on Dick's birthday to the Wyvill Arms in Constable Burton. We talked about James's A-levels and he informed his father that it was his intention to take that teenage treat, the 'gap year'.

That evening we sat and watched telly, not saying very much. It was to be the last time that James would see his father at The Parsonage.

In a major New Year's Eve avoidance manoeuvre – it was the only day of the year Dick *didn't* want to go to a party – we took off for Sao Bras in Portugal where he had bought Casa Liliana in the Algarve Hills. Richard had never really intended to buy abroad but he had taken part in the TV programme *A Place in the Sun* where he looked at various places in the Algarve pretending he wanted to.

Subsequently a friend, who was going through a divorce and needed money quickly, offered Richard Liliana. It was an old Portuguese farmhouse with small windows and thick walls which kept out the suffocating summer heat – very different from the whitewashed villas with their picture windows on the coast. But this was much more Richard's style – he preferred chicken and chips at a roadside *taverna* to the upmarket golfers' restaurants. And it would have been a good buy had it not been for the fact that, with the first rain of the season, we discovered it had a roof like a colander: we ran round the house putting down buckets and mopping up. It was like a Laurel and Hardy film and when we took in the absurdity of it we just laughed and laughed at ourselves.

We also inherited Lady Daphne Powell, who looked after the place while we were in England. Since splitting up with her baronet husband, Lady Daphne had run a cattle farm in Zimbabwe, holding out courageously against Mugabe and his thugs until they physically ejected her. No Portuguese plumber could put one over on this formidable woman.

Dick and I went for a Chinese meal that New Year's Eve – a safely non-festive thing to do since the Chinese New Year is some time later – but then we were attracted by a firework display by the sea and couldn't resist the temptation to go and stand on the beach and watch the shooting stars over the Atlantic.

Richard's old friend, Iain Johnstone – a colleague from ITN – came to stay. Richard had been Iain's best man and Iain had been Richard's at his wedding to Candy. Sadly neither marriage had lasted as long as both their TV series – Iain had devised the BBC's *Film '71*.

We went to the open-air market in Almancil where the boys bought 'Lacoste' shirts for four pounds and thick real leather belts with 'Gucci' and 'Fendi' buckles for two.

The evenings drew in early. Richard had worked out a way he could watch maybe three episodes of *Miss Marple* in succession on his new satellite system. Somehow, abroad, the programme held an extra enchantment.

We also watched Richard in a celebrity version of the BBC quiz, *Hard Spell*, which they had called *Star Spell*. He didn't want to go on it – since he made a public living from words he could have made a bit of a fool of himself. The previous year he did a 'celebrity' *Mastermind* and came last, mainly because his chosen subject – 'The BBC from 1950 to 1970' – was ridiculously wide. He had swotted up on the subject from the advent of satellite to the advent of colour but his first question was: 'What animal was Tag in *Rag, Tag and Bobtail*?' It completely flummoxed him and he never re-covered. (The answer, future BBC historians may like to know, is 'a mouse'.)

But there was a fundamental decency about Richard and he felt he should find out how it felt to be in the firing line on a quiz show, not least so that he could have greater empathy with his own contestants on *Countdown*.

I knew the result of *Star Spell* but Iain didn't and watched tensely as Dick nearly fell at the first hurdle and was likely to be ejected. Fortunately for him, Richard McCourt got in a muddle and saved his bacon. The show ended with Dick triumphantly spelling 'cantankerous' and winning the £10,000 prize ahead of Jo Brand, Penny Smith and Jeremy Bowen. He gave the money to the Cystic Fibrosis charity in memory of his niece, Alex.

He was nevertheless relieved to get back to the chair where his spontaneity rather than his knowledge was tested to record another thirty *Countdown*s in Yorkshire.

February is the cruellest month in the Dales: the winds cut into your cheeks like blades and the thick snow often made us housebound. But we were privileged and for the third winter we took off for a break in Cape Town. We rented a friend's place and lived quite simply. We liked to go to Franschhoek (the word means 'French place' since the Huguenots had settled there), where there was a shop that had the most fragrant soaps you have ever smelt. Then cheese soufflés for lunch at La Fromagerie and maybe a little wine tasting at the local vineyards.

We went to the races and also the Test match; England were touring and the 'Barmy Army' caught sight of Richard as he was leaving and broke into a united chorus of 'There's only one Richard Whiteley.' He liked that.

We knew David Gower from a previous visit, so one evening we were lucky enough to meet with him and Athers (Mike Atherton) and (Henry) Blowers in the bar and hear their amusing reminiscences.

But the high point of this holiday was a trip to Delta Camp, Okavango. From your bedroom in the safari camp you can look out over the lagoons and see crocodiles and hippos and more species of birds than I knew existed. Then, by day, you travel the waterways by dug-out canoe and watch the myriad species of antelopes and buffalo and elephants and other big game.

Richard thought that it was paradise. I would love to think that that is where he is now.

Back in Britain there were many more *Countdown*s, a few stand-in radio shows for me – and back in Portugal there was work to be done on the house. We had plans for the swimming pool which needed to be regrouted. Casa Liliana was on a hill and the garden was multi-levelled and needed much attention. We took down the pomegranate tree to create a better orchard and set in train the building of a lower terrace where we intended to install a little love seat that a friend, Sally, who was leaving for Morocco, gave us. Sadly Dick never saw it.

His 'extra-curricular' work continued apace. Perhaps at too much pace.

After a run of recordings in April, Richard went straight to Northallerton to give a speech to the Ladies Choir and present some prizes. The next day I drove him to the station and he travelled down to London for a Channel 4 lunch. That night he was guest of honour at a Cystic Fibrosis Dinner at the Royal Lancaster Hotel. He spoke, and did the auction and generally glad-handed charitable donors.

The next morning he rang Iain – they had been due to have lunch – but he said he felt so unwell that he couldn't even finish the phone call. When I spoke to him he said that maybe the fact he couldn't open the windows in the hotel had made him so hot and fluey. He was going to his regular London base, the Sloane Club, to sleep.

I suggested he come home but he had to host the Old Giggleswickian Dinner that he had organised at the House of Commons.

He managed to get through that but instead of staying for a drink with the headmaster, he took off for bed. The next morning I met him at York station. He was sweating quite a lot. We got home and he spent the rest of the day watching TV.

The following day he felt a bit better and we both did a cooking show with a chef at the Leyburn Food and Drink Festival. But, strangely for him, he cried off a friend's barbecue that night and so we just went home. I made him chilli con carne, his favourite, but he didn't want to eat. It was summer but he shivered by the fire.

The following day Dick insisted in going down to Ilkley for his brother-in-law Judge James's birthday. The house was full of old friends of his and Helen's. He had a good sense of humour and he enjoyed Maggie Marshall and the girls teasing him. 'You men can't just have a cold, you have to have flu.'

But the next day his behaviour became a little erratic. First he couldn't work out how to use his mobile phone, which he was never without. Then he couldn't operate the remote control for the TV. And then we talked about the next day's General Election and he said: 'What General Election?' This from a man who had covered them since 1966 and lived and breathed politics, and I can remember saying to him: 'Are you having a senior moment?'

I then realised it was time to stop messing about and to put Dick in the car to take him to the doctor.

He diagnosed a chest infection and because of his high temperature – which had been making him less than *compos mentis* – put him on a very strong dose of antibiotics.

Richard insisted on getting up the next day to watch the Election news on television. But he didn't get dressed and stayed in his dressing gown, which was unusual for him. He demanded his polling card because he wanted to vote. He turned to me and said, 'I need to go and vote.'

'Don't be ridiculous,' I replied, 'you can't go and vote in your dressing gown and slippers.' He didn't have the will or the energy to get changed.

That night his illness became much worse. He got out of bed to go to the bathroom but he could hardly stand. I went in to help him. I put him in the bath and washed him like a child.

I was getting more and more anxious. I telephoned the doctor who said he would call an ambulance. It seemed to take an age to come. We finally reached the Yorkshire Clinic – with me following in the car. What I didn't know was that Richard's blood pressure was dangerously low by that point and he had lost consciousness. He was given four pints of blood and he came round. I was told, much later, that Richard had had a close-run race with death on that journey.

'Don't worry,' I was assured, 'he's got pneumonia but we can sort him out.'

Paul Silverton, a cardiologist whom Richard knew, was with him and so was Richard Davison, a specialist known as an intensivist. They suggested I go home.

They rang me at three o'clock in the morning to say Richard had been taken into intensive care at the Bradford Royal Infirmary.

At 6 a.m. that morning, I went in to see Richard. He was on a ventilator with various drips going into him.

The doctor took me into a smaller room and told me the details of his illness but I could barely take them in. The trauma of having pneumonia, possibly set off by flu or maybe just a weakened defence system, had caused ulcers that had bled profusely.

I spent every subsequent day with Richard in intensive care. Judge James came to visit and Christine Stewart, who had looked after both Helen and Alex at the end of their lives, was there much of the time. Her knowledge, as a former nurse and through having a consultant as a husband, helped me understand what was happening. And her friendship quite simply kept me going.

To say the very least, Richard had bad luck. He got an infection – not MSRA – but his whole body had turned septic – most dangerously his heart. We never found out what had caused the infection.

He was sedated for the first ten days. I learnt from the consultant that for every day spent in intensive care, it took at least a week to recover. So I cancelled everything in his diary.

The infection had travelled to part of Richard's brain, a condition known as meningococcal meningitis, but thankfully it was not so severe as to cause a stroke. He was put on the highest grade of care, which meant a nurse sat at the end of his bed all the time – even when she went to the loo another nurse had to take her place.

I sat there, too, during the day, putting on a determinedly brave and cheerful face. At one time he had eight lines going into him. When he was sedated I became fixated for hours with the machines that communicated what was happening inside him, watching his blood pressure fluctuating, or monitoring his oxygen intake or heart rate. At first I would jump up when one of them went 'ping' or a connected alarm went off. Soon I learnt that this was usually the signal to change one of the drips or some other process.

The medical staff started asking me for details of Richard's relatives. When Georgina, Judge James's daughter, arrived with her fiancé Tim, they were all there. Young James, his son, was taking his A-levels in London but paid Richard a visit on Father's Day.

The hospital gave me little jobs to do like massaging his feet, swollen with the infection, to improve his circulation.

Intensive care consisted of beds arranged in the traditional Nightingale pattern. Sometimes curtains were rapidly closed round them. I had been at school at St Joseph's College in Bradford which was quite near the hospital and knew several of the girls from there who had become nurses. A greater coincidence was that the senior nursing sister in intensive care was a woman called Felicity, who had been at kindergarten with Richard where he had pinched her dolly and stuck it down the lavatory. She hadn't forgotten and teased him every day that she was going to get her own back.

'You wait till it's time for me to give you a bed bath,' she said.

Of course it was all said in good fun and it made him laugh.

After about two weeks he was moved out of intensive care and into a ward. The sedation was reduced and he was able to talk to some visitors. God knows where his mind had been during that turbulent period but one of his greatest fears was that he would lose his job as chairman of *Countdown*. I asked the executive producer, Claire Pizey, to come and see him and she reassured him that his job was safe.

Richard made a sufficient recovery to ease himself out of bed and into a chair. I read the papers to him and he listened to the radio. Things seemed slowly to be getting back to normal.

The hospital had discouraged visitors; indeed Richard was there under an assumed name – John Lee – to protect his privacy. But one day, when he had been communicating more lucidly, I called Frank and Maggie Marshall, two of his oldest friends, and suggested now might be the time to visit him.

Maggie, his late sister's best friend, did most of the talking, telling him all the latest gossip.

Richard appeared to take it in but when they left that evening he said to me, 'Have your friends gone?'

'That was Maggie and Frank,' I said. 'You know them.'

'Are they dead, too?' he asked.

I looked at him. 'Do you think you've died?'

'Oh, yeah,' he replied, almost casually.

'Well, you haven't,' I told him. 'You're very much alive.'

But it didn't sink in. 'Are you happy with what I've left you?' he went on.

'I'm happy, Richard,' I said, turning my head away so that he wouldn't see the tears.

TWO

I first spoke to Richard when I was 17. He was friendly and funny and had a winning smile. Most of all he seemed genuinely interested in me. Maybe I am rewriting history if I say I fell in love with him then. What I do know is that I loved him for most of my life. After our initial romance we were always in touch but only together for interludes, some longer than others. I had a relationship with someone in London; he lived with someone in Yorkshire and had previously been married to someone else. That is the way of these things. He used to tease me that it was like Zhivago and Lara, but the Yorkshire Dales are a lot milder than the Russian Steppes.

All my life I had been aware of him. Every evening, as I grew up, he was in the corner of our Leeds sitting room presenting *Calendar*. I must confess I didn't pay much attention and used to leave the living room when the title music came on. I preferred doing my homework in my bedroom to watching him interview Arthur Scargill or Denis Healey.

First, I suppose I should say a little about myself. Despite my name, I am a Yorkshire lass, born in Bradford. My father, Wladyslaw was Polish. He had come over here during the war to join the RAF, Bomber Command. He flew all over the place – from Bombay to Tripoli. After the war, because there was not much housing, people took in lodgers and he stayed with a couple who were to become my grandparents. When he took up with Marjorie my mother, he moved out and, quite soon after that, they married. Then came my brother Stephen and then, on 3 June 1960, me.

I first attracted attention at the opening of a supermarket in Bradford – the sort of thing Richard would perform in later years. They had run out of the proper shopping trolleys to put your baby in so my mother had to jam me into one without a seat. There was an in-house photographer there and he said to Mum: 'Your baby looks so funny sitting in that shopping trolley with all the shopping, can I take its photograph?' Then, later on, they said: 'Would you mind if we use it in a poster campaign?' My fee for that was a doll.

Some months after that they were doing another set of advertisements for Cooper's Supermarket. My mother got very excited and thought I was going to be on the leaflets that were coming through the door. She rang up the store to ask for one, telling them her baby was on the front. The manager replied, 'I don't think so, madam.' But she insisted: 'It is, it's my baby, she's on the front.' 'I don't think so, madam,' he repeated, 'we are using a picture of Rosie the chimp.' So they dropped me in favour of Rosie the chimp – early preparation for the rejections of an actor's life!

I had quite a good singing voice when I was younger and at school I would sing and act in plays. I wasn't necessarily the Virgin Mary but I sang all the songs in the Christmas nativity play. So my mother sent me to dancing class – the Jean Pearce School of Dancing in Leeds – and I was shoved in the front, not as a dancer, I hasten to add, but as the singer or the performer. They entered me for a thing called the Top Talent competition in Leeds.

Jean Pearce has launched several careers, including those of

Rosie Ford and Melanie B of the Spice Girls. She was also the choreographer of a Yorkshire Television children's programme called *Junior Showtime* and she said to Jess Yates, the producer: 'I think you should see this girl.' At the end of every programme it used to say 'If you want to audition for *Junior Showtime* write to this address', but I think I got fast-tracked through. I was immediately on as one of the kids and sang songs in what they called the finale number. I used to go on the bus to YTV. I was so thrilled to be doing it. I wasn't nervous but absolutely excited. You'd see all your friends there. We would go and play hide and seek and stuff like that. Nowadays kids are very much more mature and sophisticated but we weren't at all. We used to go roller-skating in the arena next door. Eventually the producers said: 'Would you be happy learning a script?' I said: 'Yes.' And that's how I became the presenter.

And that's when I first met Richard. I was only nine. The featured *Junior Showtime* song that week was 'Itsy Bitsy Teeny Weeny Yellow Polka Dot Bikini'. There was only one major make-up room at the studio, so while Richard was taking a briefing from his *Calendar* producer as he was being powdered down by the mirror, I was in the corner, clad only in a spotted yellow bikini, getting a body make-up.

Our show went out at 4.55 on a Tuesday evening. It was fully networked by ITV. I was at St Joseph's College in Bradford, and they were brilliant about it all. The nuns used to love me doing the telly and the show business element of it. They were very keen that I pointed out that I went to St Joseph's College in Bradford so that they could get more children on. But when I went up a year at school and the next lot of young girls came in and all started asking for my autograph, I found it excruciatingly embarrassing although my friends thought it was hilarious.

I used to encounter old film stars. My mother was very impressed that I met Margaret Lockwood and Phyllis Calvert and I think I saw James Mason once. You would see all these really quite famous people. We were very disciplined, we used to go in and say: 'Excuse me, would you mind, could I have an autograph?' And they would say: 'Yes, of course.' I think they thought we were like their grandchildren and they were really sweet to us. Margaret Lockwood used to wear a lovely mink coat everywhere.

The last *Junior Showtime* was in 1976. Curiously I wouldn't have been able to do any more anyway because you had to finish when you were 16. They were quite solid about it – 'Everybody who appears on this programme is under the age of 16.' In later years I discovered why. When you reached 16, you could no longer accept half of the minimum Equity wage; in fact Equity insisted that you get a full wage. Mr Yates, of course, would have had to make a much more expensive programme.

Actually Jess Yates was a warm and funny man and a good producer. He came to YTV from the BBC where he had worked on *The Good Old Days* and *Come Dancing*. Apart from *Junior Showtime*, he put his experience as a cinema organist to good use by hosting *Stars on Sunday*, YTV's attempt to fulfil its religious obligations in the most showbiz way possible, with bald Jess at the organ and tubby ex-Goon Harry Secombe belting out the hymns. The press gave Jess the soubriquet 'The Bishop', which probably added to his downfall when they later gleefully revealed that he had a mistress, the actress Anita Kay, who was more than thirty years younger than him. Such behaviour could not be tolerated in one hosting a 'religious' programme so he was fired and went into exile in Wales. He died in 1993 but his name returned to the public eye some years later when it came out that his daughter Paula, ex-wife of Bob Geldof, wasn't in fact his daughter but Hughie Green's. I have nothing but fond memories of him. After all, he put me on the telly.

In 1975 the film director, Alan Parker, came to Leeds to cast kids for his gangster musical, *Bugsy Malone*. I think he already had Jodie Foster as the main moll and also cast children of American servicemen stationed in England. But he had made a commercial using kids from Yorkshire and he liked the attitude of the young people. Because *Junior Showtime* was recorded in Leeds it was an obvious place to find competent dancers and singers. My chum, Mark Curry – later to present *Blue Peter* on the BBC – played Oscar De Velt, a Broadway producer, and I was his assistant. It was a thrill to be in a big studio like Pinewood, where I had my eyebrows painfully plucked for the first time. My part in the film was shot at the Richmond Theatre in southwest London. It was, all in all, a terrific experience.

I think that it was because of my role as a presenter on *Junior Showtime* that John Wilford, the producer of *Calendar* – the local evening programme that Richard presented – asked me to come and see him about a spin-off he had devised called *Calendar Kids*. It was a weird job interview: he just sat in the canteen and looked out of the window the whole time and I just prattled on. I remember going back home and saying to my mother: 'That guy's a nutcase – he didn't say a word to me.' Within an hour they had rung up and said: 'Oh, we'd like to offer you the job, do you want to come and do it? It means that you have to work five days a week, it's not just a one-off, you know, you have to come in every day.' By then I had left school and was helping out in my mother's hairdressing salon between jobs, so I said: 'Oh yes, that's fine.'

Mark was the other presenter and we worked in the same office as the news programme. The idea was to make a Saturday morning magazine show for young people, with pop music and skateboarding, and Mark and I filming fun things during the week like hot air ballooning and swimming with dolphins.

One evening before we began, Richard interviewed me on *Calendar*. 'What do you want me to ask you about?' he enquired sweetly. 'Anything except football,' I replied.

His first question was about football. I think it was a form of flirtation. We danced together at the staff party that Christmas. In the New Year he came across the office to me with a pair of theatre tickets. 'I've got these,' he said proudly. 'I thought you, as an actress, might be interested.' I said thank you and took them. He handed them over, waited, then turned and mooched away.

'Do you want to go with me?' I called after him.

It was our first date. Our friendship developed and when I was 18, and he was 34, and had already been married and divorced, we became lovers. Our difference in ages was never mentioned, but then my mother and father had a 16-year age gap.

Unfortunately for our relationship but fortunately for my career, London beckoned in the shape of the television series, *Angels*. I had done a few episodes of the unimaginatively titled *Rooms* for Thames Television – it was about single people in, well, rooms – and one of the writers, Tony Holland, worked with one of the BBC's most gifted drama producers, Julia Smith. I auditioned for her and got the part of Nurse Rose Butchins. The series was very popular but came in for some criticism because the 'angels' drank a bit and had sex – something which I'm sure nurses never do in real life.

Dick and I never lost touch, and between relationships – and sometimes during – continued our affair. He would stay with me in Balham when he came to London during filming.

After *Angels* finished I lived the life of a jobbing actress in London appearing on television, in plays and at the Labour Exchange. A more reliable income arose when I played Magda 'Mags' Czajkowski in *EastEnders*. I was Dirty Den's mistress at a time when the popular papers, especially the *Sun*, liked to cover the cast's every move so it was not unusual for me to be chased round a supermarket by a photographer.

After that bout of stardom, going back to auditions seemed like a step in the wrong direction. My father had fallen ill and I felt a need to return north, not least because of Dick. I contacted Mark Byford, who is now Deputy Director General of the BBC but was then head of BBC Leeds. I knew him and he knew my work and I was offered a presenting job with a broadcaster called Chris Ashley. We had a three-hour radio programme that was a mixture of conversation, opinion, phone calls and music.

There was also a certain amount of television. I went across to Manchester to do *Loose Women*, an enjoyable lunchtime, all-female discussion. I had a small role in *Coronation Street* and a stronger one in *Emmerdale*, in which I played a reporter. I was allowed to name her so I called her Helen Ackroyd – Helen after Richard's sister and Ackroyd after Christa Ackroyd who presented *Calendar* with him.

Richard and I spoke every day and even went on holidays to Spain and to Italy.

John Wilford, who had given me the *Calendar Kids* job, made me an offer I couldn't refuse – to do a daily three-hour magazine programme on television. It was a new cable experiment by United Artists but unfortunately it was in Bristol. The show went reasonably well, with a surprisingly good cast of authors and celebrities who agreed to be interviewed for free in order to promote their wares. But it didn't make a profit or, at least, a decent profit and closed after a year.

I was secretly relieved. I had been coming home to Leeds nearly every Friday to have dinner with Richard. Jeni, with whom he had been living, had decided to move out of his house in Burley Woodhead and, twenty years after we first met, our relationship became much more serious.

Radio Leeds again gave me some work. I didn't want to move in with Richard but remained at my flat in Leeds. I thought if we were going to live together it should be somewhere new. A friend, Paul Ashford, discovered a partly restored old parsonage in North Yorkshire. Both Richard and I knew it was right the moment we saw it and there was a sense of togetherness as we planned how best to finish the restoration and even create a pond at the bottom of the garden.

We finally moved in together in 1998 and there we lived, I would love to be able to say, happily ever after. But, sadly, that was not to be.

THREE

R ichard was born on 28 December 1943 – a war baby. In fact his father, Kenneth, had been injured in the North Africa campaign and was invalided home in a troop ship. His leg was encased in plaster and fortunately for him he fell out of his upper bunk during a storm; the plaster cracked and the ship's doctor later discovered the leg was badly infected. If he had not examined him and taken immediate action, Kenneth would have lost the leg.

But he made such a good recovery he was even able to play tennis and it was at Heaton Tennis Club in Yorkshire that he met Richard's mother, Margaret. One of his mother's claims to fame was that her sister, Barbara, was secretary to John Braine who was in the vanguard of Angry Young Men when he published *Room at the Top* in 1957.

Richard grew up in Baildon, a town near Bradford which was also home to his future co-presenter on *Calendar*, Austin Mitchell MP. Austin, nine years older, came from more humble stock than Dick whose father was the third generation to run the family worsted mill, Thomas Whiteley and Co.

Austin recalled: 'There was Upper Baildon and Lower Baildon and we were in Lower Baildon. The Whiteleys had a house on the bank that separated them so he had grown up looking down on the rest of us, literally as well as metaphorically. My father was a dyer at the dye works and Richard's came from the great tradition of mill owners. Richard was in the Wesleyan Boy Scouts and I was in the Church of England Scouts. The great dividing line was that the majority of children went to secondary modern schools, 40 per cent went to grammar schools and the elite went to public schools like Woodhouse Grove School, near Leeds, or Giggleswick. I went to Bingley Grammar School, Richard went to Giggleswick. We didn't meet the public schoolboys in the holidays because we had absolutely nothing in common. So close and so far apart. That's England.'

Richard came from fairly posh Yorkshire stock. His great uncle, Sir Frank Whiteley, had been Mayor of Mafeking, in South Africa, when its garrison under Lord Baden-Powell was besieged by the Boers for six months at the turn of the century. (Richard was far too modest to mention to the Wesleyan Scouts that he was related to a colleague of the founder of the entire movement.) It was his probable destiny to be the fourth generation of Whiteleys to run the family business. He remembers being shown round his inheritance as a small child with the weavers referring to his dad as 'Mr Kenneth'.

Summer holidays were always spent at Filey, a Victorian seaside resort popular with the Leeds and Bradford middle classes. It had none of the vulgarity of nearby Scarborough with its slot machines and dodgems; the most exciting thing to do in Filey was to follow the nature trail along the rocky Brigg or explore rock pools in search of sea creatures or – most popular of all with Richard – have picnics on the sandy beach which stretched for five miles. The high point of excitement was the Edwardian Festival when strawberry teas were served by ladies in period costume and there were barrel organs, brass bands, processions and Punch and Judy shows.

Richard was sent to Heather Bank in Bingley, a local prep school for young gentlemen where a fellow pupil, Peter

Stewart, who was a couple of years older, would one day become a distinguished urologist and the brother-in-law of Richard's younger sister, Helen. It was Peter's wife, Christine, a former nurse, who looked after Helen and her daughter, Alex, when they were dying and was to do the same for Richard.

Peter and Christine live in a lovely terrace in Harrogate on the edge of 'The Stray' – two hundred acres of glorious grass that surround the old town. The surgeon's opinion of his – and Richard's – prep school was not very favourable.

'It was a pretty crummy place staffed by masters who were either waiting to go to university or had been there and failed to get a degree,' Peter recalls. 'A bit like Evelyn Waugh's *Decline and Fall*. My parents actually took me away to sit my Common Entrance at Millfield in Somerset. I can remember Richard there – he was very thin and shy, unlike later in life. The school was at the top of a steep hill and the headmaster's monstrous wife, Ada Griffiths, insisted that boys should walk up the hill when they arrived in the morning. Those whose parents dropped them off at the door were punished. I think she's still alive, working as a shop assistant here in Harrogate.'

Heather Bank has long since closed down but it did nothing to prevent Richard winning a scholarship to Giggleswick School in 1956. He was an exceptionally bright boy and – this may come as a surprise to some *Countdown* aficionados – remained exceptionally bright until his dying day.

The sad fact was that Richard needed that scholarship. In common with the rest of the Yorkshire mill industry in the mid-fifties, Thomas Whiteley & Co. was going through tough times. Very tough times. The Yorkshire textile business was in recession due, in part, to new materials from overseas. Nylon reared its ugly head. Over the next few years Kenneth would have to lay off more and more workers until he was virtually the only one left. Richard's inheritance went out of the window. In fact he would have to support his parents in their later years when his father worked doing the VAT for a firm of surveyors even after his eightieth birthday. As Dick said to me many times: 'One day Daddy went to work in his Daimler and came home in a Volkswagen.' There was to be no fee-paying public school for Helen. She was sent to Bradford Grammar. You don't have to be an amateur psychiatrist to realise how this abrupt reversal of fortune coloured Richard's attitude to money. He always knew the value of it.

It may not have been love at first sight but Giggleswick was to become his pride and joy throughout his life. He was both proud and overjoyed when they asked him to become a Governor.

Certainly few schools can be set in finer scenery than Giggleswick in the Yorkshire Dales. From the highest point, the grand Victorian chapel, there is a 360-degree panorama of the spectacular Fells. The nearest town is tiny Settle. It was a delightful place to be in summer but less so in winter when Richard arrived in January 1957.

'The school was pretty bleak then,' said Owen Rowe, who became headmaster towards the end of Richard's time there. Even in winter, the dormitory windows were never closed: 'The snow would come in. There were fairly severe living conditions, though no different from other schools at the time.'

Although the grounds, which include the prep and pre-prep schools, are so big that you find it easier to drive rather than walk up to the chapel from the main school, the number of pupils is on the small side. With 320 pupils, it is today around a fifth of the size of Eton, and in the late fifties it had closer to 200 in number. Girls, denied access in Richard's day, now make up just over a third of the total.

'I don't know if he had an easy time of it during his first year,' recalled Derek Searle, who at eighteen was the deputy head of Shute House when Richard arrived. Richard was a bright lad and he came straight into the Fourth Form, instead of starting in the Third Form, so he was not mixing on a daily basis with boys who had come into the school at the same time.'

David Stockdale, QC, the present Chairman of the Governors, goes further: 'I wonder how much he really enjoyed it. When I was a pupil – I was in the prep school when he was at Giggleswick – it was very, very different from now: muscular, rugger-bugger. He was asthmatic, he was weedy, he was not sporty in a school that was. I come across a lot of Old Giggleswickians and they are terribly nostalgic and remember their schooldays with lots of fondness. I just wonder if he did.' Surprisingly, Richard was later to become a governor but he was never backward-looking: 'He would never, ever start a sentence with, "When I was at school . . ."' declares David. Richard did manage to keep his head above water, David adds, and clearly gained enormously from his school – however much or little he actually enjoyed it: 'He lived by his wits there, as he did for the rest of his life.'

By the end of his time at Giggleswick, Derek Searle had seen the barriers between the years gradually coming down: 'It wasn't so much in the Dark Ages by then.' It was not your age or academic ability by which you were ranked but your seniority – the year in which you entered the school. So Richard, arriving in January instead of the previous September, was at the bottom of the food chain in his class, out-ranked by (possibly dimmer) boys who had been part of the scenery for longer, although it was Richard who had arrived with a scholarship.

Peter Colman, who had been his friend at Heather Bank as well as Giggleswick, was sure that Richard took happily to boarding school life, which was not always the case: 'Some of the younger children got a bit wound-up because they were leaving home for the first time.'

'There was bullying, but only a little and Richard was never a target,' Paul Heseltine, who was a friend of both boys, recalls. 'He didn't have any enemies.' Paul was head of Shute House for a year, a position which Richard took over when Paul was promoted to head of the school. The two schoolboy bigwigs shared a study: 'A remarkably amicable time,' Paul says. 'He was extremely easy to get on with.' Richard was later best man at his wedding, an event which nearly didn't take place since Richard drove the wrong way round a roundabout when taking Paul to the stag night – and that was before the proper drinking started.

Sporting prowess was the way for boys to stack up kudos but, since Richard held the all-comers record for not touching the ball from one rugby game to the next, this was never going to be his route to the top. He used to claim proudly that he once went an entire season without any contact with the ball.

Guy Williams remembered: 'He was known cruelly as "Spasdick".' Guy was a new boy at Giggleswick when Richard was a 'Praepostor' or school prefect, and later was a new reporter at Yorkshire Television when Richard was the station's star. 'I'm not saying he didn't fit in but he was unathletic and intellectual.'

Tom Packenham-Walsh was a witness to the little sport Richard actually managed to do. 'Games were a major factor at Giggleswick and only a sick-note certified by the doctor or matron could get you off them. If it poured with rain we were organised into ranks inside the "covered playground" and performed PE for about 45 minutes in unison. If it was not pouring with rain, then we would run down to the rugby fields to take part in a game. In those days Richard had a very thin build and was not particularly tall either. Despite his asthma complaint he nevertheless had to take part in the game.

'His strategy for survival was to linger somewhere towards the rear of the field and give the appearance of guarding the back area. Should the ball perchance actually fall at his feet and interrupt the conversation he had been having with someone else, then in the face of the advancing multitude he made very sure that he gave it a mighty kick. Or should the ball happen to land in his hands from a pass, then he would quickly get rid of it.'

Richard's mother used to say that her son's games kit was a mud-free zone, thanks to his famed ability to avoid contact with the ball. While Richard might not have touched the spheroid during the actual game, the referee, Russell Harty (who was the charismatic English teacher who became a chat-show host and Richard's and then my friend in later years), would throw it at the reluctant player afterwards for him to put it away.

Paul Heseltine recalled the 'Standards' in athletics; scoring these was a way in which boys could have a shot at running different distances with a chance of achieving times good enough to score points for their house. He cannot swear that Richard managed to clock up any points in this way but he is credited for trying. In the summer, Richard was inseparable from the first cricket team, not because he opened the batting but because he was the scorer.

He had first occupied this immobile, though vital, position at Heather Bank prep school. 'He couldn't play; he was frightened of the hard ball,' according to Peter Colman, who much later presented Richard with a copy of a photograph of the prep school's 1956 team. He was going to write, 'Still scoring' on it but was dissuaded by Mrs Colman. Peter is the tallest figure standing in the back row, while Richard sits cross-legged at the front, like a small mascot.

'There was a run every other afternoon. He used to run down to a sort of barn, where Paul Heseltine kept his guinea-pigs, and hide – then run back when everyone else returned.'

Then there was – and still is – 'Scarrig', an epic race involving a quarry, a swamp and assorted peaks which Peter described as 'a mountaineering job'. Today, headmaster Geoffrey Boult remarks wryly that the sanatorium becomes uncharacteristically full in the run-up to the race.

Fortunately for Richard, he managed to get himself off games legally due to his asthma when this killer of an athletic fixture loomed over the horizon. A photograph shows him at 16 doing his first Outside Broadcast via a primitive radio transmitter, although, since the rest of the school – including masters – would presumably have been puffing over the countryside, it is hard to see who would have been listening. Perhaps he recorded it on his primitive tape recorder to play back later.

Although a conscientious skiver could keep out of harm's way in athletics, cricket and rugby, it was impossible in the school cadet force to avoid a certain amount of marching up and down, elderly Lee-Enfield rifle over shoulder. It suddenly occurred to Richard and his fellow-soldier Douglas ('Ernie') Walkden, who joined Shute House the term before, that the corps band might be a much softer option. There would clearly be no night manoeuvres, for example, as the musicians would not be able to read their music in the dark. The two boy soldiers offered their services to the 'Major' and 'Captain' in charge of the crack Giggleswick troops.

'Which instrument would you like to play?' they were asked. This was a tricky one, as playing an instrument involved certain musical skills lacking in them both. They plumped for the easy option. 'We said, "side-drums",' recalled Doug.

Reporting at 1300 hours on the appointed day, Richard was handed four drum-sticks with the little bobbles on the end. What he wasn't given was an actual drum. Then he got his orders: 'You march next to the side-drummers and if you see one of them break his stick, you give him one of yours.' This was not exactly a path that led directly to the London Symphony Orchestra. And it still involved marching. For family reasons, Doug had to leave school soon afterwards and never discovered how Richard's musical and military career progressed.

Even from the tiny images of individual boys to be seen on house photographs, it is obvious that, to begin with, Richard was the lightest chap on the premises. He was a five-stone-and-a-bit-pounds weakling, as was confirmed loudly by the PT instructor who carried out the ceremony of recording weights several times a term. Today 'Heights and Weights' is a more private individual event. Richard said he was desperate to pass on the title of Most Lightweight Person in the School and to crash through the six-stone barrier.

His eating habits were unlikely to give him the proportions of a teenage Tarzan. Schoolchildren in the Fifties were under the impression that the food in front of them was terrible, generally because it was exactly that, and Giggleswick was not bucking the trend. It wasn't so much the burnt sausages as the puddings. As yet another stomach-turning portion of stodge made its way towards Richard down the table, he employed a tip passed on by his father – which involved furtively sliding the stodgy portion into a tin and hygienically disposing of it afterwards.

This abstemious approach may have been good for his overall diet but it did nothing to boost his weight. He was still languishing at the bottom of the charts at the ripe age of fourteen and a half. Finally a tiny new boy arrived about whom Richard had great hopes. Would this small stature translate into a small weight? It did: five stone eight pounds, safely under even 'Spasdick's' last score. And on the same great day, Richard forced down the full portion of stodge at lunch, followed by three Jaffa cakes from the tuckbox. This did the trick – he was now six stone two pounds.

Derek Searle recalls Richard's terrible asthma: 'He had very bad asthma and the school had never had an asthmatic before and were fearful he might die during the night so he was put in the bed next to me and I was given the task of keeping an eye on him.

Richard suffered from such bad asthma that he sometimes had to get out of bed and stick his head out of the dormitory window in the hope that a little air would blow into his gasping lungs. Also because of his medical condition, he had a special dust-free pillow. Derek slept in a cubicle with eight-foot high walls; the younger boys were in the open dormitory. Richard was in the bed next to the cubicle, so that Derek Searle could keep an eye on him, ensuring that his head did not slip from the hi-tech pillow. Yet despite these difficulties he had an upbeat memory of Richard: 'He'd always have a smile on his face.'

Despite his problems with sport and the corps, Guy Williams recalls that Richard was very popular. Being close to Russell Harty would have helped. He adds, 'I remember being summoned to Richard's study in tears when I'd done something wrong. Richard who took his role as school prefect very seriously, gave me a firm but polite ticking off, concluding with, "Off you go, Williams."'

Day boy John Middleton, who was older than Guy and, as he put it, 'theoretically more mature', admitted to incurring a more severe punishment. Older boys were trusted to get on

with their 'prep' or homework in their studies but one evening
John was being distracted from his essay on Wordsworth's
'Lines on Westminster Bridge' by his study-mate Paddy Burns
who was, he said, 'generally buggering about'. Finally John
rather lost it. In complete silence – this was a period sacred to
the doing of prep – he tied Paddy, hand and foot, with scarves
to the cast-iron pipes running through the room.

'Paddy was trussed up like a Christmas turkey. Just as I was
attaching a third scarf around his mouth as a gag, the door
burst open – and silhouetted in the doorway was the ominous
figure of J.R.W.! [John Richard Whiteley, Richard's full
name]. John attempted some pathetic excuse but it was hard
to imagine how he could have dug himself out of trouble.
Traditional public school punishments were silly or painful or
both but Richard's was cultural: 'You will learn the poem,
and recite it to me, before you go home.'

Richard shone at the school intellectually in a way that, for
all his later success, he never did at university. Headmaster
Geoffrey Boult pointed to a subtle change which took place
while Richard was a pupil and to which he, together with
Russell Harty, contributed: developing the arts. 'It was the
idea that acting was a serious activity, that people were
reading English instead of Classics.' It was in fact Russell who
directed *The Merchant of Venice*, the first full-length school
play for many years, with Richard as his assistant. Richard
was always grateful to Russell, and to the Head of English,
John Dean, for his English A-level and S-level.

He took his O-levels (the equivalent of today's GCSEs) at
fourteen and his A-levels at the unusually early age of sixteen. He
won the Waugh English Prize and gave a paper to the school's
Basildon Club posing the question: 'Was Shakespeare really
Christopher Marlowe?' – the dramatist allegedly killed in a brawl.

It was in another field entirely that Richard was to make his
mark. Four years before his groundbreaking period as editor
of *Varsity*, the Cambridge student newspaper, Richard cut his
journalistic teeth at Giggleswick. Tom Packenham-Walsh
remembered: 'The school magazine was filled with boring
descriptions of first XV rugby matches that had taken place

and how so-and-so was now about to leave, having been captain of this, that and the other. Richard decided to publish a rival magazine and it ran for several end-of-term editions.' *An Itch of Wit* was, according to headmaster Owen Rowe, almost like *Private Eye*: 'A bit revolutionary. It was quite a new venture to have a satirical magazine.'

The launch issue bore on its cover the proud quotation 'Wisdom and Wit are little seen.' There were five editors, which worked out at one editor for every three pages. Richard was listed last, presumably because they were in alphabetical order, but, according to contributor Paul Heseltine, 'he was absolutely the driving force'.

The business side was very successful, with several advertisements from local traders. The prestigious back page was bought by K.C. & M. Pounder, area stockists for Airfix, and their proud boast was 'Balsa wood and other model supplies always in stock.'

This leading supplier of modeller's sundries was still paying up for the same slot in the Winter 1961 issue. This time the editorial quintet was not in alphabetical order and Richard moved up the pecking order to be placed third. He also wrote a comic piece: 'Quite honestly, have you ever seen a pleasant, or even a civil form?' He then produced a satirical version of the kind of boring forms we all have to fill in.

Over forty years later, Tom Packenham-Walsh, another of the contributors, remembered an occasion when Richard demonstrated his true potential as a journalist. 'One night the whole of the upper school were asked to prepare themselves for an all-out search of Ingleborough, one of the Dales' 'Three Peaks', where a party of school children had gone missing. It was like *Picnic at Hanging Rock*.' Richard's contribution to this rescue operation was to sneak upstairs to the one telephone which the boys were allowed to use – assuming that they had express permission, which he had omitted to obtain. Here he made a furtive phone call to tip off the *Yorkshire Post*. His first scoop.

Everyone said he was an unusually kind schoolboy. When Richard was a senior figure in the school, he made a habit of saying hello to the new boys, which was not necessarily the custom in boarding schools in the Fifties.

His television career was well-established when he began playing a part in the school's life again as a Governor, and this time the connection lasted for the final quarter-century of his life.

David Stockdale, who was invited to join the governing board a year after Richard, said: 'The school seems to have got under his skin. Giggleswick was like Richard's family. He didn't have the conventional wife and three children. Giggleswick became a kind of surrogate family. He would talk about the pupils as if they were his own nephews and nieces. He did not just swan around on special occasions. He pored over the pupils' exam results. He was bold when it came to spending on new schemes. He was particularly keen on the appointment of members of staff. Candidates shortlisted for the top job – headmaster – got a special treatment. Richard would take them for a walk on the lawn, stare them in the eye and ask, "Are you going to love this place?"

'He was a fantastic governor,' adds David. 'We miss him terribly. You know, I still look up at meetings and expect him to be there.'

Naturally, Richard could do the celebrity bit, too, enticing Melvyn Bragg to give a lecture, and Tim Rice to amaze the cast by attending a production of *Jesus Christ Superstar*. He organised the annual Old Giggleswickian dinner in the House of Commons, persuading Rory Bremner, a comedian who charges companies thousands of pounds for a postprandial performance, to do a turn for free. 'Richard did a lot behind the scenes,' said Giles Bowring, the Bursar. As well as the three annual Governors' meetings, there were monthly executive meetings which Richard would try to attend. 'There were financial reports three times a year; Richard didn't particularly enjoy that. He really liked projects: were we financially strong enough to modernise or start a new building?'

'As a governor, Richard relished the changes in the school,' Geoffrey Boult, the present headmaster of Giggleswick told me. 'Shute House's large dormitories with rows of beds have gone. It is now a matter of study-bedrooms, with four boys sharing in the lower age-range and senior boys on their own. There are girls, especially towards the top of the school, although they have separate accommodation. I firmly believe that the thing he loved most as a Governor was the lack of cynicism in the school, compared with the world of the media. He loved the optimism of the young people. He would have been impossible as he got older and his career wound down: he would have been here at every play and every concert! He was a great fundraiser and he gave generously of his time and own money.'

This was very true. In Richard's will he donated an enormous sum to his old school.

There was one change he did not like, and that involved the chapel. As a boy – and as a man – Richard adored the end-of-term service in which the interior of the chapel was illuminated by a single candle, by the light of which the headmaster read from the Bible on the lectern.

'He was always close to the chaplain, at school and afterwards,' David Stockdale recalled. 'He would go up to the chapel on his own and meditate. That's when he was happiest. He wasn't a practising Christian but there was a spirituality about him.'

One particularly theatrical aspect he enjoyed was the performance of a carol arranged by John Rutter at the end-of-term service; the lights were dimmed, leaving only the candles on the pillars, window-sills and altar to cast their glow over the chapel. At what turned out to be the last time he attended the service, this carol was dropped. Sitting next to headmaster's secretary, Dorothy Lambert, Richard whispered his disapproval. Last Christmas, this service was dedicated to Richard's memory.

And the candles were back.

FOUR

I n the weeks and months after his sister's death, Richard
would often sit quietly in his room neither reading nor
writing nor watching television. Just sitting. I knew better
than to disturb those silent hours but I did encourage him to
go down to Cambridge where Georgie, Helen's daughter and
Richard's niece, had returned to continue her studies at St
Catharine's College. He warmed to the idea and we set off on
a spring afternoon in May 1998.

It was not in Richard's nature to discuss the deeply personal
emotions he was experiencing. He had a fear of illness and
hospitals and death. Nor was he the sort of person who could
open up to a psychiatrist or counsellor. He internalised his
feelings in some sad corner of his soul.

In 1962 Richard had gone up to Cambridge and going back
to Christ's College where he had been an undergraduate 36
years earlier enabled him to open up about the good times he
had had there, when life had been carefree and the path before
the privileged students looked golden.

Richard had read English and pointed out that John Milton, possibly England's greatest poet, had been educated there. He was proud of some of the other men who had studied at Christ's and I have to say that I was rather impressed as he reeled them off: C.P. Snow, General Jan Smuts, Lord Mountbatten of Burma, Charles Darwin, Derry Irvine (later Lord Chancellor), Rowan Williams (later Archbishop of Canterbury) and Sacha Baron Cohen (later Ali G).

Christ's had been going since 1505 when it was endowed by Lady Margaret Beaufort, the mother of Henry VII. Sadly Richard was not to live to enjoy the college's 500th anniversary. But as we sat under the Mulberry Tree in the Fellow's Garden, I thought it was fitting that it was a Margaret, a name shared by Richard's mother, who gave the college its motto – *Souvent me Souvient*, 'I Often Remember'. It could have been Richard's own motto – he relished his past and it was, in some ways, always with him.

'Oh, crikey,' he said. 'We're in trouble.'

'What's wrong?' I asked.

'Look!' he pointed.

A red-faced man in a blazer was making his way from the porter's lodge towards us.

'We're not meant to be on this lawn,' Richard whispered fearfully, 'it's only for the Fellows.'

'Well, you're a jolly good fellow,' I teased, taking his arm. But his concern was very real, as if he had been transported back 36 years to the status of naughty undergraduate.

The man was upon us. 'I'm sorry–' Richard began.

But he was quickly interrupted.

'Welcome back, Mr Whiteley,' the porter smiled. 'We'd be very pleased if you could sign some autographs for the staff in the lodge before you leave.'

So it went on as we strolled along the Backs – the beautiful lawns that stretch down from the colleges to the River Cam. The day was as golden as the daffodils which added a note of perfection to this idyllic scene. Many of the people whom we passed would smile and say 'Hello, Richard' and just continue on their way. He had been on television most days for 17 years by then so it was not unusual for complete strangers to greet a friendly face.

Only one man, professorial and white-haired, was less warm in his salutation. In fact, he didn't make a salutation at all but merely said, with some annoyance, 'You cannot have a proper noun in a conundrum.'

'Did we?' Richard replied in some amazement. I could hear his brain ticking.

'You can hardly have forgotten,' the professor continued. 'You *are* Richard Whiteley, aren't you?'

'I am,' Richard conceded, 'but you see the programmes are recorded some time in advance and my mind has been elsewhere recently. Which proper noun?'

'That little film star,' said the professor.

Richard's memory clicked into action. 'Tom Cruise. We thought that was rather fun. Besides it's only the answer that has to be in the dictionary.'

'Which I got,' said the professor proudly as he went on his way. 'Costumier.'

We still had some time to wait for Georgie to finish her tutorial so I suggested we rent a punt. The river was filling up with them now and they looked rather stylish. A shiver ran down Richard's spine. 'No, thank you. Too much like exercise and it's harder than you think. I have a better idea.'

And he showed me some of the University's special places, like the house where his fellow Christ's man, Charles Darwin, had written *The Origin of Species*. We walked to the mathematical bridge at Queen's College which was commonly thought to have been designed by Isaac Newton.

'In fact it was a libel on him,' Richard said. 'First, he had been dead for twenty years when it was put up in 1749 and, second, it was intended that it would stay up just by the precise construction of the pieces of wood. The moment someone set foot on it, it fell into the river.'

We ended up in King's College Chapel, awesome enough without the bonus of the haunting painting *Adoration of the Magi* by Rubens. The town seemed haunted by the ghosts of geniuses.

We had arranged to meet Georgie in a nearby pub, the Baron of Beef, and she bounced into the bar like a spring lamb, so young and pretty, and so like her mother. She wanted to know how her dad and Alex were – although she phoned them every day – and Richard said that things were slowly returning to normal. The last weeks of Helen's life had, not unnaturally, been a time of quiet grief.

Word had got around that Richard was in town and an emissary from the student newspaper, *Varsity*, arrived to ask if he had time to come to their offices in Trumpington Street to have his photo taken. They were having their Michaelmas Dinner that evening and perhaps Richard would care to join them.

He politely declined, saying he was with us. But I knew that *Varsity* was part of his very being. His entire Cambridge career had been devoted to the newspaper and he had ended up as editor.

Georgie and I insisted he went, saying that we needed to have a girls talk and, anyway, we had all of the following day to be together.

It didn't take much persuasion. After he left, Georgie expressed real concern for her uncle: Helen and he had been more than close as brother and sister. He always looked to her for advice when faced with a problem and, on more than one occasion, got some unwanted advice from her. She was the only person – well, maybe me as well to some extent – who could reprimand him when he was about to embark on something that would make him look vain or silly. And now she wasn't there.

We polished off a couple of pints and then headed for Georgie's favourite Indian restaurant, the Meghna Balti House, where I fear we must have had a couple more. On our way back to St Catharine's College, by accident we passed the posh French eatery where Richard was sitting at a table with the *Varsity* journalists. Like naughty schoolgirls we pushed our noses to the window and made faces, which had the required effect of embarrassing the television star.

But not the staff of *Varsity*. All of us ended up in the pub round the corner while Richard, relaxed by now, told us all about the old days.

Alas, I cannot do justice to his tales, but on his first day at Christ's Richard found himself billeted in the same corridor as Jonathan (Jonty) Sale, who was also reading English and also had a passion for journalism which he practises to this day. He knew Cambridge only too well as he had grown up there – his father was a Fellow of Magdalene College – and, in his modest way, took Richard under his wing to show him around.

Jonty told me about their undergraduate days and in the rest of this chapter and the next he has kindly recounted his time with Richard in his own, very droll words:

'Richard used to claim that while other people got into Cambridge through the back door, he slid in through the kitchen door. This was because the headmaster of Giggleswick, Owen Rowe, came down to Christ's College in order to examine its state-of-the-art kitchens. Taking his head out of a sparkling new oven, he remarked that there was a bright lad named Whiteley whom he could point their way if they were interested.

'In fact, Owen Rowe declares that Richard was egging the pudding: "A distinct distortion," says Owen. "We were planning a new kitchen and I went to Christ's. I doubtless mentioned his name, little more."

'It was a fascinating era of change for universities, Cambridge in particular,' Jonty continues. 'In 1962 Cambridge men and women were fully engaged in the Swinging Sixties. *Beyond the Fringe*, the satirical show with Peter Cook, Jonathan Miller, Alan Bennett and Dudley Moore, had opened in London a year earlier. Also part of the satire boom, *That Was the Week That Was*, presented by David Frost (Gonville and Caius College, Cambridge), began its controversial transmissions on the BBC. On the science front, Francis Crick and James Watson had pushed back boundaries with their ground-breaking discovery of the structure of DNA and were about to be Nobel prizewinners (or, as *Varsity*, the Cambridge student paper put it after the printers saw fit to correct the front page headline, "Noble winners"). But these were all, of course, graduates.

'Back in the university itself, undergraduates still had to wear a gown when they went outside at night, on pain of a fine (one-third of a pound for a first offence) if caught "ungowned" by a black-cloaked trio who looked like Batman and two Robins but were in fact a 'Proctor' (a senior member of the university, wearing a mortarboard) and his 'Bulldogs' (college servants earning a bit extra). You could be walking past the premises where the electron had been discovered and find yourself in a time-warp facing three characters straight out of the Middle Ages. The original statutes of Peterhouse, the oldest college, had banned students from playing the game of dice. During the intervening six centuries, that rule had been relaxed but it sometimes felt as if in some ways it still was 1338.

'Richard was rather taken by all this pageantry but he was also relieved when gowns stopped being compulsory during his third year.

'Like all colleges, Christ's had a curfew,' says Jonty. 'At 11 p.m. the massive, sixteenth-century college gates slammed shut, with visitors of the opposite sex firmly on the outside. Students living in college had, like Cinderella, to be back by midnight and, for no apparent reason, the night porter noted their names and times of entry in a large book as they rang the bell for admittance and walked, or staggered, in. Anyone arriving after twelve was in trouble – or would have been if the much-loved porter hadn't recorded all times after midnight as "11.59 p.m.".

'Getting into 15th-century-going-on-21st-century Cambridge depended first of all on a 2,500-year-old language: Latin O-level was compulsory. Then there were the fiercely contested scholarship and entrance exams. And there was the back door, or, in Richard's case, kitchen door. Of those who went up to Christ's in 1962, there was at least one son and one nephew of senior members of the college. A few years earlier, a friend of ours had gone for an interview at Magdalene, a very traditional college, where he was greeted by the Master with the words: "Welcome, cousin!" He was – a cousin, that is. And he got in.

'These days, Christ's tops the Cambridge exam charts. The headline in an *Independent* article celebrating its twenty-year success referred to "the college which produced John Milton, Charles Darwin and Richard Whiteley". "Did they get Thirds too?" was Richard's amused response. In our day Christ's was known for something completely different: "rugger-buggers".

'There was a cruel joke told about the Christ's entrance procedures. When a candidate came into the Admissions Tutor's room, he would be greeted by a flying rugger ball. If the lad caught it, he would be admitted, but if he drop-kicked it into the wastepaper-basket, he would get a scholarship. The joke was in fact true, although the waste bin was an exaggeration. Since the only sporting records held by Richard involved his slowness at long-distance running and his skills at avoiding the action in school games of rugger, he would not have shone in this catch-the-ball competition. He proudly quoted Robert Morley that the only time he touched a ball was when he was playing roulette.

'Fortunately for Richard, Dr Pratt, the sports-mad Admissions Tutor, was abroad, doubtless honing his interviewing skills. (The irascible Fellow of the college was back the next year, when he had developed a new tactic: psychological warfare. "Where's your trousers?" he barked at one candidate, who immediately left the room, checked that his nether regions were in fact fully trousered, and re-knocked on the door.)

'A taciturn, and not terribly interested, scientist stood in as Admissions tutor. After leaving his charm-free zone, would-be English students were then interviewed by Graham Hough, a wonderfully world-weary don who wrote poetry and had been a key witness for the defence in the 1960 *Lady Chatterley's Lover* obscenity trial (the one in which the counsel for the prosecution asked the jury, "Is it a book you would even wish your wife or your servants to read?"). A student once sneaking into college after-hours with a girl was surprised to see Dr Hough sneaking out with a young lady.

'In 1961, the records show that only one person seems to have entered the college to read English. In 1962 Richard was one of eleven. Of these, Pat Parrinder became a Professor at Reading University. Another high-flyer was Richard Syms, who combined a respectable exam result with big roles in Cambridge plays. He became a vicar but still acts; often not just cast but typecast, playing a vicar in the Mike Leigh film, *Secrets and Lies*. Untypically, he is a drunken bum in the epic Daniel Day Lewis film, *Gangs of New York*.

'Other contemporaries and near-contemporaries included historian Simon Schama, now a professor and television's favourite lecturer, and Derry – later Lord – Irvine, who went on to be the barrister boss of Tony Blair and then the Lord Chancellor famed for the high price of his wallpaper. Naturally enough, there were sportsmen. David Rosser played rugby not just for the university but also for England.

'Richard's name, which was to become at least as well-known as any of these, was painted like everyone else's in a long list next to the door of "Y block", the building in the third court from the main entrance. The freshmen were distributed in alphabetical order, with the As and Bs starting at the ground floor. Being an S, I was next to the stairs on the top floor. Richard in the "Ws" was edged into the far corner. If he had been named Richard Zacharias, he would have been out of the college and in the street, but as it was he did rather well. By some architectural fluke his accommodation was not the usual bedsit; he had the luxury of a separate bedroom and study.

'The new buildings in the third court of Christ's were not particularly handsome but they had loos and showers, unlike some of the more olde-worlde and spectacular locations in college, where the temptation was to use your washbasin if caught short in the middle of the night. One student who did this during the bitterly cold spell of January 1963, when the River Cam was one long ice-floe on which people skated for miles, discovered his wee had frozen on the way down and his pipe was blocked until the thaw weeks later.

'The rooms had two doors, like an airlock in a spaceship. One door opened directly into the room and the other onto the landing outside, with a small space between the two for coats. When you were out, asleep or working, the exterior door was usually closed, a state known by the vaguely suggestive phrase "sporting your oak". You also might want to sport your oak if there was a girl in the room.

'Entertaining girlfriends with any degree of intimacy was a dodgy enterprise. If they stayed overnight, they would be spotted by the "bedder", a cleaner who came in every morning and incredibly, made the beds of the spoiled young students. In Richard's first week, *Varsity*'s lead story told of a freshman being sent down (expelled) from Clare College after only a few days for the crime of having a girl in his room overnight; the rumour was that the girl had stayed not for one but for two whole nights, so what did he expect? The afternoons were in general a better option for female entertainment. This did not apply to Richard, for whom girlfriends, at any time of the day or night, appeared not to be an option as yet.

'For a man described in his memorial service as a "love-god", Richard was not thought particularly divine at Cambridge. He had never gone out with anyone until he came up and he didn't spend much time on romantic assignments when he got there. This was not through choice. The odds were stacked against all male students, who outnumbered females by a ratio of around eight to one. Years later someone suggested that having to bring out his inhaler and take a pull on it from time to time might not have exactly enhanced the poor fellow's sexual magnetism. I remember him once consulting the wife of a married friend about how to pull a girl, but without success.

' "Richard Whiteley and I had a platonic friendship," recalls writer Celia Haddon, one of the most lusted-after Newnham students of her generation and today the distinguished "Pet Agony Aunt of the *Daily Telegraph*" having sold more than a million books about cats. She and Richard spent time on the student paper together. "We didn't date. At the time I was in love with and sleeping with the Arts Editor of *Varsity*, a handsome fine arts undergraduate. Richard concluded from this that I was the first woman at Cambridge on the Pill. I wasn't. I just behaved with a lack of restraint that suggested

I was! Nice girls didn't go all the way until they were engaged and maybe not even then. If they did, they concealed their behaviour. Sex was hard to get for male students at Cambridge. Sophisticated and rich young men who wanted a leg-over went to London for it, or imported rich young women without bourgeois inhibitions. Others went out with language school girls – pretty, freer because they were far from home, and, if Scandinavian, possibly more compliant. I don't remember Richard ever having a girlfriend."

'Richard nursed a secret passion for a wonderful undergraduate who was not directly named in his autobiography but was easily identified as Helen Drabble, the sister of the high-powered novelists Margaret Drabble and A.S. Byatt. She was – and presumably still is – good-looking, modest, clever and pleasant; and she was going out with someone else. Richard never gave me any clue of his obsession but he did once describe how he had just seen her and her boyfriend sweetly stroking each other's faces at a party. He gave what appeared to be an amused chuckle at the foibles of young folk but I realise now that he might well have been chuckling through gritted teeth. He would have liked to be doing some of the stroking himself.

'Richard claimed that he had gone to English Faculty lectures just so that he could admire her from afar; but, since he went to hardly any lectures, I wonder exactly how great her pulling-power was in this instance. Ironically, when he came to edit *Varsity*, his first issue contained a review of the limp film, *Sex and the Single Girl*. It was written by someone else; this was definitely not a subject on which Richard was an expert. He once conducted an impromptu survey during a party in a wood on the Gog Magog hills to the south of Cambridge (said to be the only high ground between us and the Urals, hence the cold East winds that buffeted the town). As darkness fell and we rested from dancing to a traditional jazz band that had been squeezed between the trees, Richard asked each of the group if he or she was a virgin.

'Most of us were. Richard kicked off by admitting to his complete lack of experience in this area. I joined him in confessing to a score of zero. The Newnham friend I had come with was a bit equivocal and implied that she was approximately 50 per cent a virgin, but she kept 100 per cent of the details to herself. Only one girl came out as having broken her duck. She was kind enough to express surprise at my being a non-achiever but, sadly, she did not go so far as to make the supreme sacrifice and set me to rights. And no one took Richard behind a tree either – well, not on that occasion.

'Richard did find romance in the long vacation after that party, when he went to Australia and discovered himself possessed of a certain aura of celebrity: "To think I'm in the same room as someone on *Varsity*!" gasped an Ozzie student journalist.

'A young American girl who was there was also keen on being in the same room as Richard. Unfortunately, he had to return to England and she was stuck in Australia – for the time being, at least.

FIVE

'Even if Richard had had girls to entertain, his grotty second-year digs would not be the place,' says Jonty Sale. 'No wonder he wanted to move somewhere better at the end of the year. The general rule in Christ's was that your third year, like your second, was spent in lodgings. A few exceptions were made for people running college societies. Richard, though, was not what was called "a college man". He was around for meals and would pop into the "buttery" or bar. He was perfectly sociable and amiable, particularly with a band of fellow-Northerners. He was agreeable company, generally looking somewhat amazed at whatever you told him and cautiously prefacing his own opinions with "Do you not think that . . .?".

'Yet he did not busy himself with student affairs, many of which were of a sporting nature and thus barred to someone of his abilities or, rather, lack of them. College acquaintances have no strong memories of him. One remembers Richard's tape-recorder, which was very cutting edge at a time when even my portable typewriter was considered high-tech. But, of Richard himself – nothing. Douglas Brear, another English student, remembers him mainly at meals in Hall: "We used to have white sliced bread on the tables. Richard used always to eat his slices from the inside outwards, leaving the complete square of crust." More seriously, Doug also refers to "a slightly embarrassed edge to his wit, a sort of self-deprecation".

'Former *Varsity* colleagues agree. Graham Lord remembers that, "He had a delightfully pawky, low-key sense of humour but seemed surprisingly shy and unsure of himself with his twitchy mannerisms and nervous laugh."

'Celia Haddon says: "Even then he was good at self-deprecation, the kindest sort of humour. The humour was there but it was the sly Yorkshire humour not entirely accessible to Southerners like me. Actually Richard gave me the impression of being under cover, so to speak – a young man concealing his true self, restrained, careful. If he had a Yorkshire accent, then that too was hidden from me. Perhaps the right accent mattered in the still snobbish Cambridge of the early sixties. Only later did he let the flamboyant part of his personality flower."

'It was the student newspaper, *Varsity*, which kept him away from college but it was also *Varsity* which finally got him a coveted room inside it. In his second year, Richard was sent to live out of college in lodgings. Students could live only in premises inspected and licensed by the university. Anyone who visited – just the once, generally – the house where Richard lived could only wonder what the premises were like which *failed* their official inspection. He had no access to running water and there was no question of a bath. Instead, the grumpy landlady would leave a jug of hot water and a bowl outside his door at the somewhat early hour of 8 a.m.

'At the end of his year in bath-free exile he reminded the college authorities of his involvement in the student paper. He went on to say that Graham Lord, elected the editor of the paper in the first term of our third year, was married and lived, as was always the case in those days, in a family house

Margaret and Richard, Filey, 1945.

Left
Richard and Helen, 1950.

Left
'My other car's a Triumph Vitesse'.

Above
The Editor of *Varsity*.

Above
Margaret and Kenneth Whiteley.

Below
The Mad Hatter's Tea Party.

bove
ichard with his sister Helen.

elow
he *Calendar* Crew. *Back row, left to right*: Barry Cockcroft, John
Vilford, Graham Ironside, John Fairley. Front row left to right: Michael
artington, Liz Fox, Richard, Paul Dunstan, Simon Welfare.

Left
Cathy Hytner and Carol.
'Your thirty seconds starts
now.'

Below
Richard with his PR men:
Terry Wogan and Ken Bruce

Above
My first day in Dictionary
Corner.

Below
The new look for Big Ben
didn't go down well at
Westminster.

in town with his wife and child, instead of in Churchill, his college. Graham would therefore not be able to play host to Cambridge bigwigs and important visitors.

'Being by this time deputy editor, Richard would have to take on the arduous task of inviting people round and pressing cheap sherry upon them. This, his argument continued, would only be possible if he had a decent room in college, as opposed to a hovel which was a long bicycle ride from the centre. He successfully convinced the college authorities of his plight and for his last year was back in Christ's in the third court, with a much smarter room than he had been given in his first year.

'Oddly, after all that struggle, he probably did not spend much time in this sought-for accommodation. Certainly I have no memory of ever going into it, although I spent much of my time with him. Richard and I had been thrown together from the beginning, being not just on the same corridor but also taking the same degree course. And there was another, more permanent link. At the Societies' Fair held in our first week at Cambridge, I came across the stall of *Varsity*. The Associate News Editor sitting behind it sent me off to the offices of what was, undoubtedly, the most successful student newspaper in the country. I was soon behind one of its vast sit-up-and-beg typewriters.

'Richard, though, had his heart set on television. Ever since an incident on the Moor between Bingley and Baildon when a BBC Outside Broadcast van had appeared out of the mists and summoned him like the Lady of the Lake waving Excalibur at King Arthur, he had hankered after a career in broadcasting. There was unfortunately no university equivalent of BBC2 (indeed, there was no BBC2 at all) and no Cambridge Weekend Television.

'That left the theatre, which he saw as leading to a BBC traineeship, which in turn would end up with him as the Director General. This was a great time for the Cambridge stage. Among the comics in the Footlights were John Cleese, then in his third year of the Law Tripos, and fellow-Python-to-be Eric Idle, author of the current Broadway and West End mega hit, *Spamalot*, who had, like us, just begun the English course. The very serious actor Richard Eyre, who later became Director of the National Theatre on the South Bank, was in his second year and Trevor Nunn, his predecessor in that challenging job, had only just gone down.

'All of these were hard acts to follow and Richard didn't begin to do so. He had once helped with the props for a Bradford Civic Centre production of Arnold Wesker's *Roots* and he now picked this powerful contemporary drama for his first – and, as it turned out, last – Cambridge theatrical enterprise.

'There were a number of these small-scale productions, which were put on not so much for the benefit of the audience (there might not be one) but for actors and directors to cut their teeth. Richard seems not to have got his teeth into the text: according to Richard Syms, who was in the cast, Richard W saw it as more of a social than a theatrical event. After his play had finished its very brief run, he never received a call from the Mr Bigs of student drama inviting him to take on any other production – and it wasn't just because students didn't have phones.

'Richard declared later that it was because of me that he turned to *Varsity*, the springboard to his media career. This successful undergraduate newspaper had been coming out every week during term-time for the previous 15 years. It had its own offices on the first and second floors above the British School of Motoring in Bridge Street, a marvellous central location opposite St John's College and a few yards from the Union debating society.

'Noticing that I had been getting pieces into *Varsity*, Richard thought, "If he can do it, so can I." And he could. I have no memory of introducing him to the student executives there but he said that I did. He became a reporter, and soon, despite never slipping into boots or boats, began to climb the hierarchy as Assistant Sports Editor and then Sports Editor. The News and Features editorships followed. In the second term of his third and final year he became the Editor.

'He was nearly editor at the end of our second year. In Richard's second summer term, the main competition was *not* to be editor. No one in their third – and last – term would dare to take on the onerous task at the same time as grappling with their examinations. And no one in their second year was throwing their hat in the ring. The obvious candidate was Graham Lord but he did not want the distraction of editorship while taking his second-year exams.

'Richard, the next obvious candidate, talked to Dr Lucien Lewitter who, as our amiable tutor, kept a vaguely parental eye on our well-being. Dr Lewitter's good humour was severely strained by the idea of Richard bringing out *Varsity* every week during this exam term. Richard was not, to be blunt, an academic "star" but more of a "black hole". If he got a "Special" – i.e. failed – now, he would be a big problem for the college's reputation. Should they let him back for his last year? Or just drown him in the Fellows' Pool!?

'Dr Lewitter informed Richard that if he were foolish enough to take on the editorship that summer, the college would hit him with fierce sanctions. For example, he would be gated every night at 8 p.m. Being 'grounded', as kids say nowadays, at eight o'clock would immediately wipe out the evenings which should have been spent in laying out pages and indeed would destroy any chance of turning up at the university events described in them. Listening to Union debates and going to the theatre would be ruled out. No dates, no theatre, no pubs after dinner. No evening visits to friends in other colleges. The cinema was an option but only during the afternoons, which would be crammed with all the activities Richard should otherwise have done in the evenings. Richard looked rather chastened when he came out of Dr Lewitter's room. He did not edit the paper that summer. Technically I was in the running but was not considered a safe pair of hands – by myself, let alone anyone else.

'To wrap up this story of student hacks: there was in fact a final candidate waiting in the wings, a very colourful character who supplied me, among others, with Purple Hearts, those small stimulants which I found essential to keep me awake at nights before exams while trying to learn texts which I should have learnt during the daytime months ago. For psychological reasons, he was given them on prescription and, being a generous soul, he shared them around at times of stress.

'He too had problems with exams and stayed on much longer than anyone else to pass them. When his grant ran out, he supplemented it by working for the United States Air Force, which was engaged in bombing Vietnam. His part, I think he told me at a *Varsity* reunion much later, was to get maps of Vietnam from the Geography Department in Cambridge and work out where to put USAF runways. The fact that the Americans had to use a Cambridge Geography student to position their aerodromes might have some bearing on their lack of success in Vietnam.

'Interesting though this student's talents were, he was not seen as a reliable editor but, in the absence of any another candidate, he would automatically become editor if he was proposed. Fortunately he kept well out of the way during this time of trial. The outgoing editor, Martin Adeney, who soon landed one of the *Guardian*'s coveted traineeships, chaired a crucial meeting at which we were able to change the part of the paper's constitution which barred first-year students from sitting in the editorial chair. This allowed a promising freshman to take over the hot seat.

'This was John Windsor who was in his first year at St John's but was older than the usual new boy as he had already completed a degree course at Manchester University. On graduating he went straight to the *Daily Mail*, followed by a job on the *Guardian*, and so he clearly could cut the journalistic mustard. After his summer term of editing and Graham Lord's autumn in the editor's office, it was January 1965 – and Richard's turn.

' "I'm going to start a campaign to give *Varsity* the university it deserves," joked Richard when he was elected editor. The brief announcement in *Varsity*, illustrated by a snap of Richard in an unfashionable jacket (no change there) revealed that "he is patriotic to Yorkshire and dislikes foreign food. One of the great morale-boosters in the *Varsity* offices, Richard's executive drive has helped him to edit Sport, News and Features."

'The Features Editor in Richard's term was Matthew Robinson, who later became the executive behind *EastEnders*. The weekly "Bird's Eye View" was by Suzy Menkes, who was to become the legendary fashion editor of the *International Herald Tribune*. The film editor was Brian Davis, who later edited the adman's weekly, *Campaign*. The circulation manager was Paul Whitehouse, who developed an appetite for law enforcement, ending up as Chief Constable of Sussex.

'In the first issue of that term, a Germaine Greer of Newnham College reviewed *Aladdin* at the Arts Theatre ("Widow Twankey is brilliantly played by Cyril Fletcher . . . the dancing is appalling".) Also reviewed was a new magazine entitled *Look We Have Come Through* (known to its friends on the more successful *Granta* magazine as *Look We Have Come Out*) edited by "pugnaciously obscure" Howard Brenton, whose 1980 play, *Romans in Britain*, was sued by Mary Whitehouse in the High Court over its simulated male buggery scene. Mrs Whitehouse lost, largely because she hadn't seen the play. Greer and Brenton were talented and creative but, unlike Richard, they didn't have to bring a paper out.

'Celia Haddon, the deputy editor, remembers him doing it: "I spent a lot of time with Richard in the untidy *Varsity* offices: heaps of paper, the smell of typewriter ribbons. He impressed me with his ability to plan ahead, to organise, to think things through: all the abilities of somebody with an eye for the future and with self-control during the present."

'The death of Winston Churchill inspired Richard's most powerful front page. Half of it was given over to a photograph of the statue of Sir Winston in Churchill College, with the text taken from a speech of tribute given by the Master. Richard could do serious, when required.

'One photograph showed Richard right at the centre of university affairs. "Rab" Butler, former Foreign Secretary, Home Secretary and President of the Cambridge Union and now Lord Butler, was appointed Master of Trinity and a wonderful snap showed him walking through his new empire. He was deep in conversation with a student: Richard. Richard cropped himself out of the picture when he used it in *Varsity*, so that His Mastership appeared to be striding in solitary splendour through Trinity. But Richard sent a copy of the original photo to his father in order to show him in what exalted circles he now moved. "Your hair's too long," was the main response of Whiteley Senior. He was not referring to Lord Butler. Long hair seems to have been a big thing for Richard's dad.

'For most of our first two years, we Christ's students could take a guest to dinner in the splendid Hall, where portraits of Charles Darwin and other alumni looked down on us. These guests, though, had to be male. Then the day came when Christ's flung open its Hall doors to women guests as well, a scheme which would push up the numbers and also, since the host student would pay for his visitor, the kitchens' takings.

'To celebrate the first occasion of this historic breakthrough for feminist eating, Richard and I invited two trainee secretaries who helped out with pounding the *Varsity* typewriters. (Their daily visits to our office worried their nosy old landlady, until she invited herself into the newsroom to check that we weren't a front for a white slave company.) Richard also laid on a photographer to capture the event for *Varsity* and the four of us were duly snapped, simpering in the doorway. Naturally, Richard sent a print to his father, who was impressed: "Nice girls," he enthused, adding, "but why did you take three?" (My hair was fashionably collar-length.)

'As editor, Richard pulled off another first: a colour magazine. This was unprecedented for a student paper and at the time only three national newspapers – the *Sunday Times*, the *Observer* and *Daily Telegraph* – had their colour mags. *Varsity*'s was not weekly but a one-off production. Inside its slim twenty pages was a long feature by Martin Adeney on the weight of the Middle Ages pressing down on the twentieth-century university. John Windsor opened the colleges' financial books to look at their assets, from the Trinity library worth millions to the St John's Café in Islington belonging to, naturally, St John's College.

'The cost of the first issue of the colour supplement given away with the *Sunday Times* had knocked the prosperous paper sideways. Although *Varsity* was going to produce only one issue, it could also have been affected in the same way. One of the crucial factors in *Varsity*'s success was the vast acreage of advertising obtained by Jill Platford of Educational Publicity, a London advertising brokerage company which obtained display ads – and generous amounts of money – from national advertisers and placed them with a range of student publications. An early date in the diary of a newly appointed editor was a lunch with Mrs Platford.

'"Mrs P.", formerly of the London School of Economics and older than the succession of editors parading before her every term (her first grandchild was only a year away, born, coincidentally, on Richard's birthday). "He was not my favourite cup of tea," she says, "but he was a hard worker and enthusiastic."

'"Wouldn't it be wonderful if *Varsity* could have a colour magazine?" Richard said to her. Mrs P. asked if he had any bright ideas about where the money – the cost turned out to be the then enormous sum of £1,000 – would come from. "I thought there would be enough left over," replied Richard brightly. There wasn't. The budget from the ads was expected to cover merely the normal run of the issues. A colour magazine would add extra sales but each copy sold at a mere sixpence – 2.5p – which was anyway shared with the newsagents. Extra cash would have to come from the extra ads in the proposed magazine but there was a major snag: "We already had the main advertisers advertising then anyway," Mrs. P. remembers. "I told Richard: 'I'm not going to move an inch until I know the Board of *Varsity* agrees."'

'The Board, which included responsible adults such as a senior member of the university and the boss of the printers, gave the go-ahead – provided that the ads could be found to fund it. Jill decided to try the *Sunday Times*. It advertised in *Varsity* only occasionally but, as the printing deadline loomed over the horizon, she asked some of the student journalists to lobby ex-Cambridge folk on the national newspaper. The *Sunday Times* decided to support the supplement by buying a page of space. The price still had to be agreed; and, crucially, Mrs Platford needed it to be large enough to cover the cost of the magazine.

'The *Sunday Times*' promotions manager, agreed to meet her for lunch. "Mrs Platford," he said when he arrived, "can we get the business over? How much do you need for a page?"

'The answer was £1,250, which paid for Mrs Platford's commission – and Richard's magazine. The ad was in fact for two wonderful half-pages, the first in black-and-white and the second, to demonstrate the glories of the *Sunday Times Magazine*, in vibrant colour.

'Richard celebrated the publication of the colour magazine with a lavish dinner, inviting eminent graduates of Cambridge and *Varsity* who were now in Fleet Street, such as Michael Winner.

' "Richard was delighted to get Charles Wintour, editor of the *Evening Standard*, to address us at the dinner," says Martin Adeney, "but he was very cross that Wintour didn't offer him a job." One of the reasons for the lack of job offers might have been that some of the eminent guests were rather put out to receive a bill for the meal. Some politely paid up. Others retorted by sending back an invoice "for services rendered" which exactly matched the *Varsity* bill.

'On the talent front, Oxford's student newspaper, *Cherwell*, was blessed with a column by Michael Palin and Terry Jones, who were soon to team up with John Cleese and co. to form Monty Python. On the financial side, things weren't so amusing; *Cherwell* looked pretty anorexic compared with *Varsity*. According to jealous editors of other student publications, Mrs Platford pushed more than our share of national ads our way. If that was true, we on *Varsity* did not hold it against her.

'*Varsity* was involved with the distribution of a few copies of *Cherwell* in Cambridge, while *Cherwell* did the same favour for *Varsity* in Oxford. In view of *Cherwell*'s more hand-to-mouth existence, Richard was astonished to receive a call, just before his colour magazine came out, from the Oxford paper: the impoverished Oxford hacks had beaten him to it! They were bringing out their own colour mag ahead of his. How many copies would he like? Richard was in shock. He would not be making history after all. How had they done it? The answer was: they hadn't. It was just a joke but one that worked extremely well as it gave him 24 very uncomfortable hours before he learned the truth.

'"Richard didn't like nastiness or negativity," declares John Windsor. "He recoiled from it. He was totally lacking in venom. He didn't want to cause anybody hurt – which is some people's definition of a gentleman. I remember this came out on two occasions. The first was when he felt obliged to sack a strip cartoonist during his editorship. 'The Saga of Wab' by 'Maggie', was an unfunny cartoon about a large rabbit. Richard drew deep breaths in between squirts of his inhaler; I don't think he had had to sack anybody before and the prospect unnerved him. 'Wab' ended abruptly after two issues.

'"It can't have helped that it was me that Richard was sacking," Jonty reveals. "I was fifty per cent of the cartoon, providing the pathetic speech-bubbles. The other fifty per cent was an unfortunate friend of mine from Girton who was attempting to illustrate them. Fortunately I still carried on with my day job, as it were, which was my weekly column.'

'"The second occasion," says John, "was when I unkindly nicknamed him 'Richard Spiteley' while we were discussing features with one or two other members of staff. Richard was not amused: 'Please don't call me that. It's not very nice, is it?'"

'John thinks he was not only eager to nip the nickname in the bud – nicknames can cling to you for life – but also simply found the name unpleasant.

'"He did seem to have a deep-seated sense of reap-as-you-sow and do-as-you-would-be-done-by," says John. "His kindness to others was innate but I think he also reasoned that if he were foolish enough to hurt anybody, he would get it back in full measure, one way or another. So he never did – hurt anybody, that is. As a result, he never made any enemies and I suspect this may have been true of the rest of his career."

'There was one small episode in which Richard did blot his copybook but he could argue that he was led astray. Graham Lord has joyful memories of how "a baying mob of Pitt Club arseholes threatened to throw Norman Lamont and Christie Davies through the plate-glass window of the British School of Motoring." The Pitt Club was a young gentlemen's establishment for aristocratic undergraduates and was situated round the corner from *Varsity*'s offices above the BSM premises. (When I had lunch there, one of the other guests was a sixteen-year-old Lord.) Christie Davies was a lad of the centre-left and thus the natural foe of drunken toffs, especially when they were dressed in eighteenth-century outfits, as this lot for some reason were. (They may well have thought it was in fact the eighteenth century.) But these Pitt Club posers were so extreme that someone like Norman Lamont, a Thatcherite even before he became Margaret's right-hand man, seemed to them to be practically a Commie.

'Fortunately the two Union bigwigs (smallwigs, in the case of the diminutive Christie) sought sanctuary in the newspaper premises. Here they took their revenge by joining Richard and Graham in inkbombing the sozzled aristocrats all over their white, eighteenth-century ruffs.

'By the time Richard had put his last issue to bed, the summer term and our Finals were only weeks away. One of the wonderful aspects of the Cambridge system was that, as well as lectures, students had "supervisions" in which they were taught singly or in pairs. During our three years, we had been going to supervisions together or, in his case, *sometimes* going to supervisions together. While he was tied up with *Varsity*, I would cycle off to the supervision or seminar with an oral sick-note. "Richard is not feeling too well," I would say. "He's at a family funeral," was another excuse. This was true but not every time.

'One of our lady supervisors did not have the privilege of actually meeting Richard during the entire year when she was supposed to be teaching him, until I finally led him to her house and introduced them. "I've brought a friend," I said. She didn't complain about his previous absence but was thankful that he had finally made it.

'This is not to say that turning up at supervisions had got me very far. One of our – or, usually, my – supervisors was supposed to be a recruiting officer for the British security services. The spymaster, if he was one, never asked Richard or me to be a double agent or even a single agent. Presumably he decided that, since we had trouble finding his room on time or bringing a coherent essay with us, we were unlikely to be much use in following the nuances of the Cold War.

'Richard Axton, then a young research student who had just started teaching us at Christ's, fished out for me the exam results for the summer of 1965. In the Finals, Pat Parrinder – now Professor Pat – was one of only ten people in the university to achieve a First in English. Two students at Christ's managed a very respectable Upper Second and two a more disappointing Lower Second.

'Back in our first year, only a couple of Christ's students had disgraced themselves with Thirds in English: Sale and Whiteley. At the end of the second year, there had been only two Thirds: Sale and Whiteley. And now in the Finals, there were 33 English students in the entire university who ended up with Thirds: they included Sale and Whiteley.

' "Special Prize for Consistency: Sale and Whiteley!" laughs Dr Axton now.

'Since I ended up with the same lowly degree as Richard, I might just as well have gone with him to the printers and given our suffering supervisors a few afternoons off. Richard learnt more from the exam debacle than I did. Having seen rather more pretentious films than him and read rather more pretentious books, I rather fancied myself intellectually. But I heard him say, in his down-to-earth way, "I'm not an intellectual: I've got three Thirds." '

SIX

As Jonty Sale has so vividly recalled in the last two chapters, Richard's time at Cambridge represented a turning point in his life. In the Sixties only about ten per cent of young people had the good fortune to go to university and, unlike today, they could almost choose from a wide range of jobs on offer. If you had been to Cambridge and edited *Varsity* the world of journalism was wide open to you. Richard was offered a job on the *Daily Mail* but since childhood he had been passionate about television so he eagerly accepted a traineeship at ITN.

In some ways Richard was fortunate to get in. The editor, Sir Geoffrey Cox, was a very short New Zealander and usually hired very tall people such as Andrew Gardner, Peter Snow, Gordon Honeycombe and Sandy Gall, all of whom were well over six feet. When asked about this unusual method of recruitment, Geoffrey would say that he remembered his days as a scrum-half back home and it was the tall, second-row forwards who protected him in the line-outs.

Richard – five foot nine – was not, however, engaged as a newscaster but to learn to be a sub-editor and scriptwriter for the news bulletins. His first day in July 1965 provided a shock. His fellow trainee was none other than Michael Morris, former editor of Oxford's *Cherwell*, who had perpetrated that nightmare prank on him by pretending that he was going to bring a colour supplement out before *Varsity*. Richard did not forgive easily and the froideur between them never thawed into friendship.

That apart, Richard loved being in a newsroom full of the famous newscasters and reporters he had watched as a child, none more so than Reginald Bosanquet who made little secret of the fact that newsreading was hardly a real job and could even be done while sloshed – something he demonstrated on memorable occasions.

Richard's job was to be given a piece of 'wire copy' from Associated Press or Reuters and turn it into a brief news item. He graduated from the odd football result to racing where, as he loved to tell people, such was his ignorance of the sport of kings that he wrote down the odds of the winner of a big race as 8–2. Amazingly this was broadcast even though there are no such odds – they would be 4–1. Even more amazingly the 8–2 statistic wasn't even referring to the odds: 8 stone 2 pounds was the jockey's weight and ITN was besieged by hundreds of calls from bewildered punters. He managed to hold on to his job – just – and, later in life, became a successful owner with his horse, the Mare of Wetwang, outclassing the field in a ten-furlong handicap at Ripon.

His *Varsity* chums had also sailed into jobs in journalism: Celia Haddon on the *Daily Mail* – when she got her first by-line Dick was extremely jealous – Jonty Sale on *Queen Magazine* and James Wilkinson as assistant to the super-sleuth Chapman Pincher on the *Daily Express*.

He and Jonty rented a friend's flat in Battersea for the summer, the only downside being that it came with a Harvard student who could communicate only in grunts. Jonty remembers they used to call him the 'Boston crab' – but only behind his back.

They were just across the Thames from the King's Road where the Swinging Sixties were in their infancy and these two bespectacled Cambridge nerds would take a bus across the river and stare at the trendies, knowing that they could never aspire to such glamour.

In the autumn they moved to a tower block in Notting Hill Gate. Alas, this was 35 years too soon to be fashionable as Hugh Grant was, at the time, only five years old. The flat was a sub-let from another media man, Tony Palmer, who had distinguished himself at Cambridge by composing an opera in Greek and, in later life, by directing a film about Wagner with Laurence Olivier and Richard Burton, which ran for nearly eight hours. His etiquette, however, did not always match his talent. At the top of the block, occupying the 17th and 18th floors lived the legendary *University Challenge* quizmaster, Bamber Gascoigne. Jonty already knew him as he had been a student of his father at Magadalene College, Cambridge. To impress his friends Richard invited both Tony and Bamber to a party and was proud to introduce the two men – 'Tony Palmer, meet Bamber Gascoigne.' Tony shook the quizmaster's hand and then turned to their host with the words: 'I've met him. Can I go now?' Richard always said that he wanted the earth to swallow him up at that moment.

Jonty remembers Notting Hill as being a great area. 'The Tube was a few yards away, with the Central, Circle and District lines. From the living-room window we could see the queues at the art-house cinema over the road and could note when it was time to whip down and join them. Kensington Palace Gardens was just down the road. However, the rent swallowed half our salaries after tax, quite apart from a standing order we signed to pay for the previous tenant's furniture. ('What you don't have you won't miss,' he remarked consolingly about these regular deductions from our bank accounts.) In addition we were paid, like everyone else, after we had done each week's work, while the landlord required his cash an impossible three months in advance. As the weeks wore on after the date when the rent was due, the landlord would send us a reminder. Finally, just before the date for the next lot of rent, our three cheques would be popped reluctantly into the post. That third cheque was from Patrick Eagar – another *Varsity* man who went on to become Britain's leading cricket photographer – who fortunately took the remaining bedroom and made the whole dodgy enterprise remotely possible.

'Richard and I were both addicted to the box and hated switching off when the last programme ended. We were thrilled to notice that after one of the channels closed down, you could catch test programmes transmitted in colour. They were not, of course, received in colour by our standard back-and-white set. These were purely experimental transmissions for the benefit of a handful of television engineers working on the colour transmissions which were still in the future as far as ordinary programmes were concerned. They consisted mainly of Part One of an elderly film about pirates. We watched this for several nights, thinking it seemed a bit familiar, but never caught Part Two. What we did once glimpse was a studio programme in which the emphasis was clearly not on content but on having someone who would sit still in one place while colour cameras were pointed at him, or them in this instance. Two supermarket under-managers were having a cautious discussion about the finer points of filling shelves. The item should by rights have been sponsored by Horlicks but Richard and I were thrilled: this could be our chance to perform on the box.

'We came up with the idea of writing to the producers of this slot and suggesting that we could fill it rather better. We would (a) sit down and (b) talk while (c) cameramen gained valuable practice by working out how to stop the strobe effect on Richard's jacket. The fact that we had nothing to say would not bother the handful of insomniacs and engineers and cat-burglars who would be our only viewers. BBC2 had recently started screening *Late Night Line Up*, the lively arts programme which introduced Joan Bakewell to the nation and ran until, in the words of another presenter, Sheridan Morley, it had interviewed everyone in Britain at least twice. Yet *Line Up* was not planned originally to be anything like as elaborate as this. Run out of a broom-cupboard, it was supposed merely to provide continuity announcements telling viewers about the next programme; then it took off. Sadly, our idea had nothing in common with *Line Up* except that it would have been aired at a time when nobody had anything else to transmit.

'Richard typed out a very neat proposal for our project, which had the modest working title of *The Nightly Whiteley Show* and would have involved two smart young men, i.e. us, talking about the week's news. The idea was not green-lit by television executives nor even amber-lit. The fact that he did not send the letter was just one of the reasons for this. If we had in fact made a programme, and if a TV bigwig had seen it, Richard's television career would have been entirely different, in that it would not have existed at all.'

Worse was to happen at ITN. The aforementioned Sheridan Morley – son of the film star, Robert – had worked there as a sub-editor but also read the late night news bulletins when the tall men couldn't do them. He had defected to the BBC and a new man was recruited to do the job. He was the same age as Richard and had just left Bristol University. Iain Johnstone had managed to talk himself into reading the news on BBC's Points West while at that redbrick institution which was also attended by Geoffrey Cox's twin daughters. They told their father about him, Geoffrey needed another newscaster in the build-up to the 1966 General Election, auditioned him and gave him the job. Richard was livid; Johnstone wasn't even tall. He resolved never to speak to the newcomer.

Richard once came back from a late shift and woke up Patrick and Jonty from their doze over the news, telling them that he had bumped into Norman Lamont, later Chancellor of the Exchequer, in the street and asked him up. They regarded Lamont as unbearably pompous and whipped upstairs to bed. Richard had to pretend that there was no one at home, leaving Lamont to deduce that the flat was haunted by a ghostly bath-runner and loo-flusher. Over the years he usually tended to ask Norman to his parties, which may have been out of guilt.

Jonty further recalls: 'After a couple of years in Campden Hill Towers, Richard began to be affected by the style revolution sweeping the country in the late Sixties. "The trouble with this place," he declared in a lordly way, "is that it's got no ambience." In fact, the main thing wrong with the visual attractions of the place was the pink nylon shirt which he insisted on wearing. His solution to the ambience deficit was to get some large candles and stick them on the mantelpiece. "There we are," he enthused, leaning back to survey the room by the light of the gentle, flickering flames. "Ambience!" That was when he leaned back too far and his shirt caught fire and was ruined. Still, it was the pink one, so there was no harm done.

'The typewriters did not help the décor much, either. In those days they tended to be found mainly in offices but we had three in the flat, a fact which did not escape the plain-clothes detectives who banged terrifyingly on our door in the early hours of one December morning and declared that they had just received a report that an armed robber had taken cover in the flat above the shoe-shop. "Lot of typewriters," one of the coppers, who didn't miss much, said cunningly, hoping to trap us into admitting that "yes, we ran a stolen typewriter warehouse." I explained that we were all journalists. His face fell. It fell more when we pointed out that it wasn't ours but the flat below which was immediately above the shoe-shop.'

'Ruinously expensive though the flat was, it enabled Richard to find for me – quite by chance – what he could not find for himself: a wife. After we both moved out, one of the vacant rooms was filled by Ruth, the sister-in-law of a contemporary of Richard's at Giggleswick and Christ's. Richard rightly claimed credit for being a matchmaker and kept a proprietorial eye on our relationship. We should have had an official stamp on our marriage certificate: "This wedding is sponsored by Richard Whiteley, OBE." Sadly, Ruth died a few weeks before Richard from a brain tumour.'

In his second year-long vacation from Christ's, Richard had spent a month in Australia where he encountered a species that was fairly new to him: girls. Just as Jay Gatsby had attracted hordes of women to him because he was an 'Oxford man', Dick managed to have some success in that department because he was a 'Cambridge man'. In his diary for that year he records how, in Brisbane, he met Rosemary for lunch and Veronica in the evening of the same day. He later revealed that it had been an American girl there who had introduced him to making love. Veronica later came to London in pursuit of him but she was not quite as he remembered her.

However, Richard's flame had been lit and he lived exactly opposite Notting Hill's equivalent of today's Singles Bar, 'Big Mary's' Launderette. Evidently you could put your washing in a pillow case and hand it to Big Mary and she, for a shilling, would do it for you. But those on the prowl would sit for an hour and watch not only their washing go round and round but also the young female singles of the borough who had come with something similar. Thus Richard met a stunning French girl called Monique Ruffaut who was looking for somewhere to live and he persuaded her to take a room in his apartment. Sadly, for him, not *his* room. But they became friends and he became a great deal more gregarious.

Monique was a little eccentric. She announced one morning at breakfast that she was no longer Monique Ruffaut. Henceforward she was to be known as Monique Tascher de La Pagerie. Dick used to say it reminded him of the Knights who say 'Ni' in Monty Python and the Holy Grail. They changed their name to the Knights who say 'Ekki-Ekki-Ekki-Ekki-Ptang. Zoom-Boing. Z'nourrwringmm.' He subsequently discovered that Tascher de La Pagerie was the maiden name of Josephine who married Napoleon Bonaparte so possibly Monique wanted an injection of aristocratic blood. They lost contact but Richard and I bumped into her in a Chelsea chemist, of all places, many years later. She was rather cold to me and took Richard to one side, saying she wished to speak to him in private. After she'd gone I asked him what she had wanted. He said she had instructed him never to say to anyone that they knew each other when they were both 23 or otherwise people would know her age.

I think it was the experience of working late nights together on the 1966 General Election programmes that dissolved Dick's animosity towards Iain Johnstone. After all, Iain had done him no wrong – unlike Mike Morris! By then Richard had met Emma, a graduate of Exeter University who had some sort of job in publishing, and Iain had an on-again off-again relationship with a girl called Renate who had been at Bristol University with him.

'They were rather similar women,' Iain recalls. 'Very dominant characters. Remember, the Pill had just become generally available and women's lib was in the air and Germaine Greer's *The Female Eunuch* was just around the corner. I think Richard met Emma at a party. I seem to remember her still wearing braces on her teeth. I also have an image of her ironing his shirts while she was in her underwear. She said she always liked to iron in her underclothes. Anyway we all decided to go on a short holiday together and Richard, with great originality, suggested a motoring tour of the Yorkshire Dales.

'We both had Triumphs – mine was a Triumph Spitfire and his a Triumph Vitesse with a smart pair of slanting headlights on each side. Anyway we might as well have been on mules for all the good these sporty engines did us because Richard had to be in front as he knew the way – or did most of the time – and his glasses weren't really suitable for driving so he rarely exceeded twenty miles an hour. It must have been spring and the snow was still in the hedgerows but, for some perverse reason, we both had the roof down and it was numbingly cold. We couldn't wait to get to whichever hostelry we were spending the night at and plead for hot baths. I remember we had "borrowed" the AA book from the ITN library to find such places and the mild-mannered librarian, Lew Gaeschlin, went absolutely berserk when we finally returned it.

'On some days, if there had been a bit of arguing or whatever at breakfast, the girls would take my car and Richard and I his. He had bought this wonderful tape which you plugged into your machine and a man described the various places of interest on the journey – "on the left you can see Jervaulx Abbey, built by Cistercian monks in the twelfth century, just ahead is Middleham Castle, home of Richard III, now you are crossing the River Ure . . ." Only we weren't. Because the tape was for people travelling at 30 mph and we were doing 20. But Richard loved it because the chap who devised this ingenious tourist vademecum was not too keen on doing much research and got round it by saying things like: "You are now passing a ruined tower – many people have wondered what this was" and then moved on. We laughed a lot.

'Sadly things didn't work out between him and Emma and she went off and married a man called Marshall Stewart. Or maybe he was just called Stewart and Marshall was his Christian name. Many people have wondered which.'

'The following year we went skiing in Saas Fee. I'd been before but Richard joined the beginners' class. I was skiing home at the end of the first day and found Richard, at the bottom of a slope, poking around the snow-covered river-bed with his pole.

' "I'm looking for my ski," he said.

' "Didn't the instructor ski after it and stop it?" I asked.

' "He did the first two times," he replied.

'A strange thing happened on the first day of that holiday, the sort of thing that hot-blooded young males dream about. Murison Small, the tour operator, had organised a large party on the night we arrived – about a hundred of us spread over ten chalets – along with the departing hundred whose bedrooms we would occupy. A girl came up to Richard and said: "Do you know, you are the only man in this room that I fancy." She was Susan, a nurse from St Thomas's in London.

'Dickie couldn't believe his luck. When he abandoned skiing, which was about day two, Susan stopped as well and they went on long mountain walks together, holding hands and doubtless staring into each others' eyes. On the last night there Richard asked me if I could find a spare bed somewhere else in the chalet as he thought it was time he and Susan went to bed. In the middle of the night I felt a tugging on my pyjamas. "You can come back to the room," he said. Sadly Susan didn't think it was time.

'But fate moves in mysterious ways and when it was our turn at the end of the fortnight to pack our bags for a 4.00 a.m. plane there was another of these mass parties. Richard was dancing with one of the ladies who had arrived. Both of them were pretty drunk and she suddenly said that she wanted to take a look at her new bedroom, would he come. Which he did. Once inside she locked the door and didn't turn on the light. They kissed.

' "I'm going to take off my clothes," she announced, making for the bed.

' "Isn't it a bit soon?" he asked a little nervously.

' "You don't know London girls," came the confident reply.

'Soon he did. On another skiing trip – well, walking in his case – we met a girl called Rusty and vied over her affections.

'Richard played a trump card back in London, taking us to the Boat Race and wearing his Cambridge scarf to impress her. I am not an Oxbridge man. He found a pub in the AA book – his own this time – which had tables by the river. They were sparsely populated and as we ordered our third or fourth beer Richard called to the landlord, "What time does the race pass here?"

' "It ends half-a-mile downstream, sir," came the reply.

'Things sort of worked out between me and Renate to the extent that we got married and Richard was best man. Somehow, because the marriage was subsequently dissolved, so is the memory of the ceremony. I wonder if that's a common psychological trait. It took place in a village church in Wheeler End in Buckinghamshire. I cannot remember a word Dickie said in his speech but I do recall he performed a valiant service in almost putting my mother's anxieties to rest because Renate was German-born and mother had not completely absorbed the fact that Generaloberst Alfred Jodl had signed an unconditional surrender to the Allies in Reims more than twenty years previously.'

Shades of Basil Fawlty in years to come. Iain later partnered John Cleese in writing a movie, *Fierce Creatures*. I remember the three of us coming home from Middleham Stable Day one Good Friday and slumping in front of the telly to watch the film. Dick, who was well-lubricated from the hospitality of the various trainers, clapped a hand on Iain's shoulder and said in his usual assertive way: 'Now I want you to tell me all the behind-the-scenes details. Which lines Cleese wrote and which lines you wrote.'

Before the opening titles had come to an end he fell into a deep and contented sleep that lasted well past the closing titles. That's what friends are for.

SEVEN

After Richard had been at ITN for a couple of years, it was announced that the northern ITV region held by Granada was to be divided into two, so Leeds viewers would no longer have to put up with Manchester news. Various consortia were formed to compete for the franchise which was won by Yorkshire Television with the editor of ITN, Geoffrey Cox, as deputy chairman. This was a double incentive for Richard to return to his roots where he would be a bigger fish in a large but not national pond. Geoffrey recommended him to Donald Baverstock, a volatile Welsh man who was leaving the BBC, who saw Richard and suggested to the Managing Director, Ward Thomas, that they hire him. Which Ward did with the words: 'Welcome to YTV, David,' a name which he continued to call him for many years and Richard was too shy to correct him.

Richard was delighted and Geoffrey Cox was pleased, too. 'We will walk down the Kirkstall Road arm in arm together,' he told his proud recruit. Kirstall Road, in Leeds, is where YTV was and still is. But initially the company occupied the premises of a former trouser factory. Richard joined in April 1968 when he was 25 and formally left 35 years later when he was 60. By then YTV had been swallowed up by Granada, although the local news kept its separate identity. With perfect symbolism for him, the YTV chevron was erected on the front of the building the week he arrived and taken down the week he left.

There was a tremendous excitement about the place with a bunch of young people – some journalists, others trained in television and radio – brought together to put on the nightly show, *Calendar*. Despite his tender years, Dick was one of the most experienced, having worked on the ITN coverage of the terrible Aberfan disaster of 1966 when a hill of slurry had enveloped a Welsh mining town killing 144 people, 116 of them children. In those pre-digital days videotape was two inches wide and edited by slicing it with a razor blade. For the young scriptwriters at ITN it was a sad but pressured learning curve.

Richard's main job on *Calendar* was to be a reporter. The studio anchors were Jonathan Aitken, later to find fame as an MP and infamy as a jailed perjurer, Michael Partington and Liz Fox. A little later along came the experienced Austin Mitchell, now MP for Grimsby. Geoffrey Cox encountered him at a dinner in Oxford and when he learned that Austin had experience of current affairs television when he was an academic in New Zealand and was also a Yorkshireman, despatched him to Baverstock immediately.

'Jonathan Aitken, the main presenter, used to stare at the camera like a rabbit caught in the headlights,' Austin recalls. 'He shouldn't have been on the programme at all because he was a parliamentary candidate but Baverstock didn't worry about such things. However, after about six weeks, the Independent Television Authority caught up with him. Actually ITV was on strike when I joined but I still got twelve pounds a day as we recorded stuff at Batley Variety Club. I almost immediately got addicted and stayed. Richard was the most welcoming when I arrived. I was a fellow university chap and we were both Baildonians.

'I think my experience in New Zealand made me more relaxed in the studio because the autocue wouldn't work or the film insert broke and the Chroma Key which was meant to throw up images behind me used to be very erratic. There was me, taking over from Jonathan, Michael Partington – Mighty Particles – who was very smooth and the most experienced of us, Liz Fox with her short skirts – she was attractive, vivacious and a marvellous television presenter and Richard, who was still the aspirant candidate, always wanting to climb the ladder and get himself on screen. He was mainly outside on film but he would fill in. He had a very polished background from ITN. Richard used to try and humanise stories and make them humorous. He was a very serious journalist when he started out, so he had to adjust to a more populist medium. We all did.

'Donald Baverstock initially wanted the programme to be like *Tonight*, the Cliff Michelmore BBC current affairs programme he devised with Antony Jay and Alisdair Milne. When the Soviet Union invaded Czechoslovakia in August 1968 Donald devoted the whole of *Calendar* to it – experts on Czechoslovakia and Poland, a former ambassador to Moscow, deep analysis of our relations with the Soviet Union etc. It was mad, a real audience-killer. I liked Donald but he could be very erratic in his judgements.'

Richard used to tell me how Donald, at the morning meeting, would say things like: 'I was reading a really interesting article on Kierkegaard in bed last night and I woke up Gill (his wife) and I said "We really must do something about this on *Calendar*." '

I later got to know Donald and Gillian Baverstock because their daughter Sara was in my class at school and, despite Gillian's vast inherited wealth – she was Enid Blyton's daughter – they made me very welcome at what was known to the local taxi drivers as 'Noddy Hall'. I remember a teacher walking into our classroom one Monday morning and demanding: 'I believe we may have Enid Blyton's grand-daughter in this class. Which one of you is it?' But Sara refused to reveal her identity.

Calendar became infinitely more popular and accessible when Donald concentrated more on his job as Director of Programmes and *Calendar* was left to John Fairley, John Wilford – who hired me and Mark Curry for *Calendar Kids* – and Graham Ironside.

Graham recalls: 'Richard had two great strengths, and he had them in spades: he had stamina and perseverance. He just battled on, week in and week out, proving his competence and his commitment, until it became crystal clear that he had more than a spark of skill and originality. But all the while, he felt that he was like the kid with his nose pressed to the sweetie shop window as others slipped into the anchor's chair, or moved on to new, more prestigious programmes and jobs. I know he longed to be one of the main presenters, and could hardly hide his dismay when newcomers arrived on the scene, potential competitors for the top slots.'

John Fairley, who oversaw the programme, remembered the day Dick was sent to Leeds Market where, a researcher had discovered, there was a butcher still selling horsemeat, a story thought to be one which would intrigue *Calendar* viewers. Richard's report gave all the essential details – how long the business had been running, where the owner acquired his supplies, who his customers were, etc etc. And it ended with this tailpiece: 'So here are the choices for today's discerning shopper: stew at £1.50 a pound, steak at £2.20 a pound or you might like to try this. It was at 10–1 at Wincanton yesterday. But it came last.' Incidentally, my dancing class was two floors above the horsemeat shop.

Graham Ironside recalled that Richard was not always as witty when faced with the live thing.

'His skills and expertise in rural matters, in truth, seldom held up when put to the test by real sons of the soil. Richard would have hated to miss fronting our coverage of the Great Yorkshire Show and the Lincoln Show, both big "hardy annuals" in the *Calendar* News Diary but he probably did his best work signing autographs and lunching in the President's Hall, while others dug out the stories of the day. Come programme time, and confronted by a series of agricultural items to report, his body language clearly betrayed his innate distrust of anything four-legged, hairy, furry or smelly.

'On a glorious June afternoon at Lincoln Show, he had to interview the proud owner of the Supreme Champion bull, a muscle-bound Charollais with malevolent red eyes and a pair of testicles so enormous they scarcely cleared the ground.

'From the off, he was struggling. The farmer was one of the laconic variety and parted with words sparingly. All Richard's questions were used up in the first 40 seconds of the interview – and he still had a minute to fill. In his desperation, out came the classic ". . . Er, em, so tell me, what kind of a cow is this?" They're still laughing about that one in North Hykeham.'

Marilyn Webb, a junior reporter, remembered her very first day on the programme:

'I was sent as Richard's shadow to Hull where he was to meet up with the local film crew to cover a dockers' strike. These were days before the M62 and the quickest way to Hull from Leeds was by train. I don't suppose Richard was particularly pleased about having to drag me along with him, and it showed. The journey took an hour and for most of the time Richard remained engrossed (hidden) in the *Guardian*, both there and on the way back. The only conversation was when I ventured a question or two. He was very polite – but it was hard work. In later years, as I got to know him better, I put it down to shyness – but I won't say what I thought at the time.'

Marilyn, an attractive blonde with a warm girl-next-door persona was later to co-present the programme with Richard for several years until she fell in love with the YTV gardening correspondent and went off to tend his plants.

Another of Richard's fellow reporters, I remember, was the exotic Edwina Tarporley who had a rather pronounced lisp with her 'r's coming out as 'w's. The news desk would compete to find her assignments where this could be used for maximum entertainment value, the most appreciated being her report on the Rank cinema chain.

Richard would, from time to time, either read the news – nearly everybody in front of and behind camera read the news at some stage in their careers – or do the occasional studio interview. He was also a third string to Austin and Michael on political spin-off programmes, politics being his speciality.

'We did do a serious weekly political programme,' Austin recalled. 'It started as *Yorkshire Matters* and became *Calendar Sunday*. It was a three- or four-way discussion. There were over 60 MPs in the YTV area but most of them were too stupid to appear – or too drunk. It was primarily Particles and me who presented and occasionally Richard, who later took it over. Certainly he was a regular at the boardroom lunch before the programme. Peter Tapsell, the member for Louth and Horncastle, always wanted to be flown up by helicopter. He was a successful stockbroker and he used to give us tips over lunch such as "buy gold!"

'Denis Skinner, the former miner from Bolsover, wouldn't eat in the boardroom. He went to the canteen and paid for his own meal. The third time he was on I did manage to persuade him to come up to the boardroom. He tried to give Sir Richard Graham, our chairman, sixpence for coffee.

'Richard was seriously into politics and very early on went to all the party conferences. I don't think he had any ideology – but he liked politicians.'

Eventually, time and toil brought Richard the prize he coveted. He left behind his days as a roving reporter and his seemingly permanent place on the subs' bench and, at long last, he became one of the studio presenters. Julie Mews, who now lives in Australia with her husband Nelson, was their assistant.

'All the programme production offices were still in the old Trouser Factory,' Julie recalls, 'and one of my earliest memories of those days is of literally *running* the green copies of the nightly *Calendar* script over to Studio 2. The yellow News I & News II were run-over later. The studio PAs were always bribing the secretaries to get the scripts over as fast as possible because the programme was really chaotic in those early days and every minute before 6.00 p.m. counted. An early script made the life of the studio PA so much easier because then when the late changes happened, she was at least organised.

'When we moved over to the new building I sat at a group of three desks with Richard, Mighty Particles and Barry Cockcroft, the main documentary director. Austin (who was very untidy and therefore needed two desks) sat next to us on the same side of the office and opposite Barry. We had such fun. I couldn't believe that I had got this job and was surrounded by people who wanted me to do it well.

'After the morning meeting I'd help Richard and Michael to set up their assigned studio interviews, type early versions of the links scripts, do their expenses (I have to say with Barry's ex-Granada experience, and Michael and Richard's ITN experience, doing their expenses was a steep learning curve for a girl like me). After the running order was done, I'd then help type the main script. As soon as the green script was delivered to the studio and the technical areas, it was my job to greet the studio guests in Reception, take them to the Green Room, let Richard and Michael know who had arrived, take the guests to make-up and generally hang around the Green Room, trying to be useful. I completely fell in love with the whole scene and always stayed until after the show and had a drink with Michael and Richard.

'In the office, Richard was always incredibly kind and helpful to me. He certainly "marked my card" for me, always telling me what to do and when. Richard treated everyone with the same courtesy, whoever and whatever they were. He influenced my attitude to work for the rest of my life.

'Many of the people in the office simply had no experience of television at all. We were all incredibly young (I was 20 when I joined *Calendar*) and all terribly excited to have the opportunity of working in a new television station. There was a huge enthusiasm and keenness about the place. I think we ran on that, adrenaline and fear.

'When I think about it, 38 years later, I can see how Richard very cleverly carved a middle-ground for himself on the programme in those early days, falling midway between Austin (always fooling around) and Michael Partington – (dry, nearly always deadly serious). The more Austin fooled, the more Michael tried to nail the Headingley Councillor to make him change his mind on air about some bad Council decision, the more Richard strove to find ground of his own. By doing this, Richard didn't have to compete with Austin and Michael; he was doing his own thing. And he made sure that what he was doing was not something either of them were doing.'

When Michael Partington left the programme to go to Tyne-Tees Television, Richard joined Austin as co-anchor.

'We both valued the partnership,' Austin told me wistfully. 'We may have been competitors but we liked each other and got on. Presenters are always kept hungry by producers. They treated us like children with toys so we were both in it together. Every one of us wanted to do every item. While we would compete for the crumbs to be dropped from the table, we were a team. I liked to go off and make films about go-go dancers but Richard had an almost unhealthy respect for the good and the great and would do interviews with people like Denis Healey and Tony Benn.

'We were always on the look-out for different ideas. I remember Barry Cockcroft, who used to delight in making Yorkshire films about the Dales and Moors, instituted the World 'Knur and Spell' championships on *Calendar*. 'World' was a bit ambitious since it was a game that was only played in the Barnsley area in the early part of the last century. The Knur was a small ceramic ball, also known as a 'Potty' because it was used to stop limescale furring up kettles. It was released when your foot pressed a sort of lever on the ground – that was the Spell. Then you had to see how far you could hit it with a stick – the Pummel. Somebody hit it nearly three hundred yards. Barry persuaded Lord Kagan to sponsor the Championships for a couple of years and Richard and I and all involved got free Gannex raincoats.'

Various colleagues said they were impressed to see how urgently Dick seized the programme running order as soon as it was printed every afternoon.

He confessed to me all he wanted to read were the first two items:

Item 1 – Opening Titles
Item 2 – Opening Link: Richard Whiteley

Graham Ironside revealed: 'When I became a regular producer, I worried long and hard about writing the presenters'
links. While they had to convey important information to the
viewers sharply and incisively, they had to sound reasonably
intelligent and fairly like something Richard himself might
say. Alas, all too frequently, after the transmission, we often
had to have sharp discussions as to why Richard had departed
from my carefully honed scripts. But no matter how I ranted, I
seldom extracted anything like a coherent explanation. It was
only at his memorial service that a co-presenter from those
early days gently let me into the secret. Richard's eyesight was
so poor that he couldn't always read the autocue. Vanity
stopped him from wearing his specs on camera, and from
admitting his problem, but it also honed his ability to ad lib, a
skill which saved both our skins on more than one occasion.

'About the same time, Carol (Vorderman) told me something else I hadn't quite realised: she assured me Richard never
understood anything anyone Scottish said. Shame. My accent
had been acquired in darkest Aberdeenshire and had hardly
been modified, in spite of 40-years' exposure to exile in
England.

'We both got our adrenaline fired up by deadlines and being
live. Crises and emergencies were a speciality. We had our
mettle truly tested one night in the mid-70s. At about 6.15,
roughly halfway through *Calendar*, from Master Control,
came a squawking noise on talkback. And that was alarming
because that never happened during a live transmission:
"Could the producer please call Master Control *urgently*?"

'I called. It was one of the senior Transmission Supervisors,
David Dale, a cool-headed pro of long experience. "Now,
Graham, we're not panicking yet but there could be a little bit
of a problem down the line . . ."

'It was *not* a little bit of a problem. One of ITV's endemic
industrial disputes had broken out at ATV in Birmingham
whence, as a rule, issued forth the nightly soap, *Crossroads*,

at 6.30, straight after *Calendar*. Except that tonight, it was going to be delayed.

'Since *Calendar* was a live slot and we journalists were always greedy for airtime, perhaps we would like to fill in a little time? Just till ATV can deliver tonight's episode to the waiting nation? Anything to oblige, David.

'More by good luck than good judgement, we had a "stand-by" item available, so, with all the confidence of the blissfully ignorant, I happily promised to fill another few minutes. But, at 6.32 or thereabouts, it became clear that *Crossroads* would not be transmitted that evening and blank screens would appear imminently unless . . .

'While the stand-by item ran, Richard and I had a hurried conference: we can fill till seven o'clock, can't we? Yeah, sure.

'Good old Whiteley! Not only did he know everyone who would be in the bar that night – Julia Foster, John Stride, as well as half the cast of *Emmerdale* – but as we were about to find out, he'd clearly memorised from the current *TV Times* the complete career and personal history of the delicious and charming Miss Foster.

'Seconds later, she and John Stride, slightly bemused, but still clutching the G&Ts they'd so recently been hoping to enjoy, found themselves ushered into the *Calendar* studio, seated beside the imperturbable Mr Whiteley. And, for the following 20 minutes, the viewers were entertained to a riveting chat about Miss Foster's starring role as the "angel" in *Mr Axelford's Angel*, a recent YTV production and Emmy winner in New York.

'Thanks to Richard's quick wits, his encyclopaedic knowledge of show business and of "our" stars at Yorkshire TV, they heard, in extensive detail, several anecdotes about the making of *Wild Alliance*, the series in which she and John Stride were currently making in a neighbouring studio. And suddenly, it was seven o'clock and Yorkshire Television was able to resume normal service.'

Dickie's paranoia took another hit when he was told that Bob Warman, star presenter of ATV's local news, was to join YTV, eventually to work on a new breakfast programme that

Paul Fox, who had arrived from the BBC to run the company, wanted to pioneer. Richard desperately wanted to do the job but probably was lucky not to, since it disappeared into oblivion as they filled the show with old episodes of *Peyton Place* which someone must have bought in a job lot. So Bob, an experienced presenter, joined *Calendar*.

In later years they became the best of friends and Bob, his wife, Di, and Dick and I would take holidays together. As I said, Richard and I spent his very last Christmas Day at the Warmans and they came to stay with us in South Africa the year Richard died. But it wasn't always that way.

Bob shook his head as he thought about his early days with Richard: 'I first clapped eyes on Ricco in 1976 and it was an unfortunate start that we had because unbeknownst to me, my arrival had been flagged up by the then editor as the arrival of a new presenter who was going to bring a fresh look to *Calendar* and all this sort of nonsense. I came from ATV in Birmingham. When I walked into the *Calendar* newsroom I met with a very frosty reception from my later-to-be friend Richard. So much so that he didn't speak to me at all for months, although we sat next to each other.'

It was a shared phone that eventually broke the ice. John Willis, Yorkshire Televison's BAFTA-winning documentary maker about social issues, gave the instrument its name.

'Even though I was making these documentaries,' John explains, 'you didn't get a bloody office, mate. You just had a desk in the newsroom. Actually I quite liked it because making documentaries can be quite lonely and, because I had worked there, I knew everyone in the newsroom and I was quite happy in there. I was somewhere between the presenters and the sports desk. So even though I was making some hard-hitting documentary about poverty, on the one hand I would be answering the sports-desk phone and writing down who would be the subs for Sheffield Wednesday next Saturday and then I would answer Richard and Bob Warman's phone and it would always be some girl. So I would have to say "Sorry, he's in make-up at the moment – what's the name?" So I dubbed it the "sex phone" and that it remained.'

Bob remembered it well; how could he forget it? 'We had this phone in the middle of the desk and we did have shared interests in enjoying ourselves and the love of women. John Willis said there's the sex phone going again so I used to start taking a few of Richard's calls and Richard used to take a few of mine and we started to almost share each other's women. Nevertheless when I left in 1979 he was very, very relaxed about it. Our friendship only really blossomed from that moment.'

I also had a desk in that long newsroom to prepare for *Calendar Kids* and, when I embarked on this book and spoke to Bob about it, I confessed to him that I used to be scared of him.

Bob was genuinely amazed. 'Heavens above, if I had known that people were scared of me I would have really used it to my advantage. Do you know, in a rare moment of communication at the time, Richard once asked me: "Who's that blonde in the corner?" And I have to admit I said: "Just some irritating girl who is doing a children's TV show."'

That was me!

EIGHT

At school, when he became a senior boy, Richard was renowned for the care he took to ease newcomers through their early days – perhaps remembering his own nervousness back then. At *Calendar*, when he became a star presenter, it was no different. Before he made his name as a documentary producer John Willis, son of Lord Willis who wrote the legendary *Dixon of Dock Green*, was a young new boy on the programme. John and Janet Willis were to become great friends of Richard and me – and remain so to this day.

'I was starting on a three-month contract as a researcher,' John recalls. 'I had come up from London and I had never been to Leeds in my life. No one knew me from Adam and here was this kid from London who didn't know his Sheffield from his Barnsley working on the news desk. That first day Richard came over and said, "I'll take you down to lunch." He and Austin were the stars of the show and he didn't need to do that to someone on a three-month contract. He knew I was on my own – I didn't know where the gents was, let alone where the canteen was. I was staying in a boarding house and in the afternoon he said, "I think I know the person who can find you somewhere to live." And Julie Shaw (later Julie Mews), his PA, came over and said she thought she knew of a place and then took me in a cab to a building where I found a flat straight away. He was not to know at the time that when I became Director of Programmes at Channel 4, 24 years later, I was able to double his salary by doubling the number of episodes of *Countdown*.'

From my seat in the Newsroom I could observe the controlled chaos that was *Calendar* as Mark, myself and David Lowen, the producer, worked on the script for *Calendar Kids*. John, later a big cheese at the BBC, had a wonderfully wry eye on what was happening in his new environment.

'It was a really exhilarating place,' he recalls. 'Every day you had fantastic fun. Everything was possible. It was incredibly creative. It was full of amazing, larger-than-life characters: Richard, Austin, John Fairley, Sid Waddell. But they were very professional. You learned from people. It was a fantastic training ground. We made sure we were first with the news. One day we'd be covering the explosion at the chemical reactor at Flixborough where 28 people were killed. On another I remember we were all given Spanish sombreros and castanets and the programme went out with half the production team on the screen. I can't even recall the story but there was often this strange, quirky sense of humour. And it worked.'

Richard was not above the odd practical joke. After he died, Sheena Hastings, who had been a researcher on the programme, wrote in the *Yorkshire Post* how she came back from lunch and Richard had left a message on her desk to ring Mr C Lyon who had an interesting story for her and giving his telephone number. She dialled it and became red-faced and furious when she realised it was Knaresborough Zoo. She looked across at Richard and he was wet-eyed with mirth.

Because Richard had Yorkshire blood coursing through his veins, he was never slow to spot a story that brought together luminaries from the county. Julie Mews observed that.

'In 1970 Richard did his wonderful two-handed filmed interview with Vic Feather, then General-Secretary of the TUC, and Barbara Castle, then Employment Minister. Richard – and this was typical of him – had discovered that the two of them had been childhood friends in Bradford, going to the cinema together and, later, to Labour Party meetings. Richard sat Barbara Castle and Vic Feather down on the sofa of her old home in Bradford (he had even persuaded the present owners to lend their house for this filmed interview.) The edited film ran for about 20 minutes and it was wonderful to see these friends and sometime adversaries reminiscing together. It was rather like a filmed version of *Desert Island Discs*: a non-confrontational interview allowing the participants to reveal far more of themselves than they would in a studio. At that time in *Calendar*, only Richard would have persuaded the Cabinet Minister and the top Union Leader to do it.'

Although the oldest person there and an Oxford academic, it was frequently Austin Mitchell who had the most offbeat ideas. One night he persuaded John Fairley, the editor, to begin this news-orientated programme with a tribute to Bob Dylan – who hadn't even died.

'Well, he had been out of circulation for a long time after a motorcycle accident and made his first public performance at a tribute concert to Woody Guthrie,' Austin argued. 'So I arranged for an elaborate sequence of photos and images to be cut to his song "Nashville Skyline" with me between them giving a live narration. It was an absolute disaster. None of the pictures came up on cue and those that did fell off their primitive stands. A nightmare five minutes. John Fairley just gave me an old-fashioned look when we came off air.'

On occasion the items on *Calendar* might have been more appropriate for *Calendar Kids*. There was the famous night when Austin, Michael and Richard were all involved in the studio. Austin had been sent off after the morning meeting to an auction of police stuff, presumably to find something funny. He came back into the office having bid and got 100 police whistles.

Live on air he sat on a stool in the middle of the studio, brandishing one of them.

'We all know what happens if you blow a whistle,' he began – and blew it. The director cut to a library shot of a policeman walking towards camera. 'Along comes a policeman . . .'

'But what happens if you blow 100 police whistles?'

The vision mixer was meant to cut to a shot of a baby elephant being walked across the shot (the circus animal had been hired by Jess Yates for *Junior Showtime* and was hanging around in the scene dock beside the studio).

Right on cue, when the vision mixer cut to the elephant, it was being manoeuvred backwards through the Studio 2 door and both its bodily functions went off at full blast all over the place. Austin fell off his stool laughing and there was nothing to do but carry on with the programme. The next item was Michael doing one of his very serious interviews.

There was the most incredible row in the office afterwards. Austin still laughing hysterically and Mighty Particles nearly having a heart attack, saying How Could He Present a Serious Programme etc. etc.

Richard tiptoed to his desk, put down his script and tiptoed down to the bar to keep out of the row. He never got himself into a position where he had to take sides with Michael against Austin or vice versa.

There was another terrible row, much more justified, at the very end of the programme one night when Austin was given a newsflash to read about an IRA hunger striker, Frank Stagg, just having died in Wakefield Jail. The next (scripted) thing to happen was Austin having a custard-pie thrown into his face for some reason or other, followed by the closing credits. In the row that took place in the office after the programme, Michael was almost speechless with anger and decided, perhaps understandably, to move to Tyne-Tees television.

Michael, another Yorkshireman from Harrogate, had actually interviewed Richard on Anglia Television about his *Varsity* colour supplement. It was he who had suggested that the awkward undergraduate should have a go at television and was a source of wisdom when they found themselves together on *Calendar*. Michael died the year before Richard.

In effect, this left the programme to Richard and Austin. It wasn't all custard pies and elephants. John Willis observed: 'Richard and Austin were very astute political interviewers. They were very passionate about Yorkshire but also very passionate about politics. They could go from high level politics to fairly low level stuff. I watched Richard go from being a rather boyish-looking slightly nerdy young man into being a fully formed television personality who somehow just fitted the screen. He had a fantastic passion for television. I don't know anyone else who would know the directors of every programme, who the lighting cameraman was on documentaries, the set designer, the history of television. He just loved being on the screen.'

Richard and Austin were both happy to use their television fame for a little extra-mural earning: 'We both used to do personal appearances, things like presenting bingo cheques or opening a new Woolworths,' Austin recalled. 'There was an agent called Carl Gresham who fixed these things and we would get about a hundred pounds for doing them. I don't know how much Gresh got. He also used to supply people to *Calendar*, like Alexandra Bastedo, and at Christmas we would get Gresh-style cards and badges. He certainly lightened our lives.'

'To begin with I always regarded Richard as rather shy, especially with girls. The idea that he was the great sex god is totally wrong. Over the years he became sophisticated and confident. He had this gleaming Trumph Vitesse. He mixed with everybody and he knew everybody, he certainly knew who was shagging whom and had a unique sense of humour. When I was up for selection as a Labour candidate he didn't want me to succeed so he poured a bucket of water over my head on the programme the night before to make me look foolish.'

Richard loved Austin and was devastated when he finally was elected to Parliament as MP for Grimsby and had to leave the programme. It was like losing an elder brother, he often told me, although the two kept closely in touch.

Richard teamed up, rather reluctantly at first, with Geoff Druett, a political journalist and interviewer with a distinguished career history at Tyne-Tees Television and later, at Anglia.

Geoff, who was to take charge of Richard's funeral and memorial service, had a very original take on Richard's on-screen performance.

'Richard, on location, seemed to have television luck – whether it was that hotel in Scarborough which conveniently collapsed behind him into the sea just when we went on air, or being in the Grand Hotel in Brighton when the bomb hit. In each case he had the skill to make them exciting stories. Even the notorious ferret that bit him on *Calendar Tuesday* – an afternoon show. Painful, yes, but the way he dealt with it live on air turned it into a classic piece of television.'

The gist of Richard's encounter with a ferret – which over the next thirty years was to become one of the most popular clips on TV outtake shows around the world – is as follows. On *Calendar Tuesday* in 1977, while handling a ferret during a live studio interview with its owner, the animal, unconvinced by Richard's charms, abruptly turned on him, sinking its needle-like teeth into his hand and held him there. Meanwhile the ferret handler advised Richard, ferret dangling from his finger, to put her down, and blithely reassured him that the ferret would not hurt him, to which Richard replied: 'But she *is* hurting.' He then endured half a minute of agony before the pair could be prised apart. During the ensuing commercial break, a YTV nurse rushed to the studio and told Richard to take his trousers down for a tetanus injection, which of course he did. The incident was to haunt Richard throughout his life – to comical effect, needless to say – and even a few weeks before his death Richard reflected ruefully that the *Yorkshire Post* would probably report 'Ferret Man Dies'.

Geoff and Richard did a political programme every Thursday evening, usually from London. Graham Ironside was impressed by the manner in which they built up respect on both sides of the House and even from some individuals normally thought to be 'difficult' by members of the media.

They were, of course, subjected to a constant stream of criticism by Denis Skinner, MP for Bolsover, who, nevertheless, contrived to appear on *Calendar* regularly enough to ensure that his constituents, heartland viewers of Yorkshire TV, remained aware of his presence.

Tony Benn, then MP for Chesterfield, but still living in Bristol, frequently left home in the wee small hours in order to travel to Leeds to record an interview and immediately travel back to the House of Commons for the start of business. He said it was 'because we always get a fair hearing at Yorkshire'.

Even Denis Healey, now Lord Healey of Riddlesden, whom Richard found intimidatingly intellectual and certainly the most unforgiving to careless questioners, was a generous and amusing guest, in spite of his merciless teasing. Off-screen and at social gatherings, he confessed his respect for Richard's interviewing skills and his affection for Richard, the man. When he published his first book of photography, *Healey's Eye*, it was Richard who spotted the opportunity to make a half-hour programme about Denis's childhood around Keighley and Bradford.

Despite his less than welcome reception from Richard, Bob Warman has always respected his talents in this direction.

'I always had an undying admiration for Ricco's contacts – the number of people he knew and he really did know these people, particularly in showbiz and on the political front. Fantastic. I don't know anybody nowadays working in regional television who had the sort of contacts that Ricco had. He was passionately interested in TV, he just loved the business, more than I have ever done. Really I regarded it rather cynically as a business over the years but for him it was a passion. He just loved broadcasting. He just loved television. He also knew a lot about politics and he developed those two interests to a great degree and these people in both spheres of television and politics knew that Richard was an expert in both. He really did know an awful lot about television and he knew an awful lot about politics so he was well respected on both fronts.'

Richard adored the Party Conference season in October. There were opportunities to meet old chums from ITN and to joust with competitors from the BBC. There were opportunities to meet the movers and shakers from the constituencies. And there were opportunities to pick up ideas and tip-offs for future programmes.

He loved politics and politicians. He loved the big set-piece speeches and the debates and he loved to be at the centre of decision-making, to watch history in the making. He also loved the receptions, the press conferences, the lunches and the dinners. And, most of all, he loved the intrigue, the gossip – and the cocktail parties.

'I found it almost impossible to keep up with Richard when we were in London for the political programme we did or when we were at the three party conferences,' Geoff confessed. 'After work he used to rub his hands together and announce, "I'm IPM", which meant "in the party mood". He seemed to know everybody. I would find myself in amazingly posh houses like Laura Sandys, Duncan Sandys's daughter, who was a high-powered political consultant and prospective Conservative candidate for South Cambridge. At the conferences, long after I wanted to go to bed, he would drag me along to another party for another drink. He had quite amazing stamina. He would come to breakfast the next day looking like death and by midday he would have a glass in his hand in preparation for a good lunch.'

Back in Yorkshire Richard Madeley, later to find fame and fortune as Richard of Richard and Judy, came on board as a new reporter. Unkind souls said he made a point of always calling Richard Whiteley 'Dickie' so that he would be the only Richard on the programme but that is unlikely since he was very much the junior citizen. He, himself, recalled: 'After I had failed to rattle a dodgy councillor during an interview, Richard leaned across to me and said: "A touch too much hairspray, old boy."'

A new female presenter was recruited to dilute the all-male club. Christa Ackroyd was an executive, running Radio Aire which had its HQ next to YTV and was reluctant to swap that for the less secure position of being on-air talent. 'I said to boss Richard Gregory, I am not interested in TV because all that happens is Richard does politics and Geoff does politics and all your woman does is read two minutes of news and do the story at the end about ducks or the Women's Institute. At the time I had done the Hillsborough Disaster, Bradford City Fire, the Ripper, and I felt I was really a much more hard-hitting journalist than that kind of face. But he promised me faithfully that it would be different.'

It was. Christa and Richard formed a powerful partnership which was to last for his final seven years on the programme. She was the daughter of a Bradford policeman, had joined the *Halifax Courier* from school and was a true news hound. And she was tough.

'When the Gulf War happened in 1991, Richard Gregory asked me if I would mind not doing the programme that night, because he thought it would be better that two men presented it. I said: "Oh, because women won't be interested in the fact that we are at war, is that what you're saying?"'

She did the programme.

'Richard taught me the most important thing, he may not have voiced it this way, but he believed that *Calendar* was showbiz. It was a performance, it was a programme and he taught me to value half an hour's nightly airtime. There are people who would say he didn't differentiate between a network programme and half an hour in Yorkshire. In fact, quite the reverse. He would say: "But everybody watches *Calendar*," and so he almost made it more important because he was broadcasting to his own.'

Graham Ironside invited Richard to present what he considered to be among his finest hours in the *Calendar* stable. 'The squabbling sisters of ITV set aside their competitive instincts to mount a Television Telethon, a massive charity event, based on the Jerry Lewis Telethons in the USA. It would take place on Bank Holiday weekend in May 1988, starting on the Sunday evening at seven o'clock, and running through – non-stop! – till ten o'clock on the Monday night. Michael Aspel would present the first 20 minutes of each hour from

London and then hand over to the regional companies, each of which would then present their own 10-minute segments.

'The six months leading to the Telethon became a frantic haze of planning, pleading and persuading people to undertake all kinds of crazy fund-raising activities, from bathing in cold baked beans to building a sheltered housing estate for elderly couples. When I eventually had a running order roughed out in my head – three, four and sometimes more, items per segment, with live interviews, news reports and Outside Broadcasts timed to the second – I thought the time had come to start briefing the presenter, on whose shoulders would fall this Herculean task. Ever the thoughtful producer, I invited him to a favoured haunt, Betty's in Ilkley, for coffee and toasted teacakes, essential rations for such an Everest of an undertaking. Sheaves of scribbles in hand, I started, painstakingly, to recite the masterplan in fine detail.

' "So, while Jimmy Savile rallies the troops in Studio 4, you can do a couple of interviews, so that'll give us time to switch to the OB at Castle Howard . . ."

'In minutes, I became aware that Richard had glazed over and was devoting most of his attention to his Fat Rascal. (For the uninitiated who have never had the good fortune to visit the Broad Acres, as Yorkshire is sometimes known, Fat Rascals are based on an old recipe from Turf Cakes. When Yorkshire bakers finished for the day they mixed all the leftovers together and then gave them to farmers up on the moors to bake over a turf fire. When the Swiss confectioner, Frederick Belmont, came to England to seek his fortune, he was fascinated by the style of Yorkshire baking. He took the Turf Cakes, filled them with currants, mixed rind and almonds and decorated them with cherry eyes and split almond teeth. He thought they looked like cheeky little rascals and so the Fat Rascal was born. Richard was, to say the least, partial to them.)

' "Look, old boy," he said. "I *am* listening. Sounds as if you've thought it all through and I trust you. But, look, if we have 20 minutes between each segment, you can tell me what to do in the next segment and I'll just do it." End of briefing. And that's more or less what we did.

'When we arrived at work that Sunday morning around eleven o'clock, the studios were already as busy as a beehive. Every scrap of space was occupied by activity of some kind. On the lawns in front of the studios, a funfair was poised to go into full swing. In the car park, people were already starting to queue for admission as audiences. In the studios, bankers were firing up their computers. Telephone engineers were checking a thousand lines. Technicians were wiring in every switch and cable in the Northern Hemisphere.

'Throughout the next unremitting 27 hours of technical rehearsals and transmission, Richard gave the performance of his life – interviewing an unending human stream of fund-raisers, accepting huge cheques and buckets of cash; linking to a bewildering series of outside events; announcing the running totals as the funds rolled in; building up the excitement to crescendo after crescendo.

'The programme went like a dream. The money poured in like a lottery roll-over. It ended in an emotional explosion of tears and triumph. We were high for a week. For that alone he deserved the two consonants and a vowel which later came his way.'

Ferret aside, Richard's finest *Calendar* achievement was that he was the first reporter on the scene in the middle of the night of 12 October 1984 when the IRA bombed the Conservative Conference hotel in Brighton. The YTV film crew had gone home so he commandeered a Southern TV film crew and set about reporting the biggest story of his career.

The sight of Richard, shocked and covered in choking dust, delivering a piece to camera in front of the wreckage of the building was one of the most memorable images of his time at *Calendar*.

When he eventually arrived back in the office, he was met by a spontaneous standing ovation by his colleagues in the *Calendar* newsroom. That was probably the first time he realised the respect in which he was held by his colleagues – but, of course, that didn't mean they'd miss the chance to tease him.

Later, in the bar, having taken a refreshment or three, someone asked him: 'OK Richard, great job, but what were you really doing there at three in the morning?'

Quick as a flash – before he could reply – one of our worldly-wise women producers snapped out: 'What do you think? Just the usual – chatting up some bird.'

On his way back from Brighton Richard had a duty to perform in London where Iain and Mo Johnstone had asked him to be godfather to their daughter, Holly. The christening was due to take place in St Columba's Presbyterian Church just near Harrods but, beforehand, assorted friends and relatives assembled in the garden of the Johnstone's Fulham home to wet the baby's head.

Richard, dust still on the shoulders of his suit, the hero of the hour, was regaling them with tales and details of being in the thick of things when Holly's other godfather arrived. It was Andrew Neil, then the Editor of the *Sunday Times*. He had been at the hotel, as well.

'Hi, Richard,' he said, 'what a night!'

Just as waiters in restaurants ask for the order at the moment when you are about to deliver the punch-line of your best joke, somebody always turns up to spoil your story.

NINE

Ten years after he had left home for Giggleswick in 1958, and then on to Cambridge and then to London, Richard returned to his parents' house at 6 Greencliffe Avenue, Baildon and his own bedroom. Margaret, his mother, had always kept it ready for him and he had been a dutiful young man, returning for holidays and Christmas.

Kenneth, his father, was still working – albeit no longer as boss of the family business – and his younger sister, Helen, was in her last year at Bradford Grammar School. She had always lived at home and was a lively, commanding presence in the household. Richard was slightly in awe of her personality and wit and had proudly shown her off to his chums at Cambridge, one of whom had taken a keen interest in her, but not one that was reciprocated.

He drove to work every day in the 'Trouser Factory' in an unglamorous grey two-tone Ford Anglia that he had bought from his mother. Richard was on a salary of £2,600 which made a 24-year-old pretty well-off then, especially if he was living at home and had already mastered the art of submitting expenses for his initial work as a roving reporter. Few restaurant meals had to be paid for out of his own pocket.

And there were quite a lot of them. With its bevy of bachelor scriptwriters and directors and reporters and a complement of pretty PAs and secretaries, the staff club at YTV in the early days was something of a singles bar. He remembered Carole Tudor from his schooldays – although she, at first, didn't remember him.

'In 1968 I took up residence as the (rather tarty) secretary/receptionist in the Sheffield Office of Yorkshire Television. Richard was on some reporting job in the area and came into the local office, to check me out as I had been mentioned in the *YTV News* that month.

'He asked me if I knew who he was and yes, I'd seen him on *Calendar*.

'Richard replied, "And?"

'Blank face from me.

' "Don't you remember?" asked Richard.

' "Remember what?" I replied.

' "I met you at our School Dance . . . at Giggleswick. I escorted you into dinner and we danced together."

'I remembered the dance as it was the very first time that the two single sex schools of Giggleswick and Casterton had been allowed to meet up for a whole evening – escorted by a large army of moth-eared teachers who were there to make sure that no mischief came about. I had to admit that I had no recollection of him, but I told him that I used to keep a diary at school – as most of us did in those days – and if I had met him, then surely his name would be mentioned. And there it was (still is) in schoolgirl script on a Thursday at the end of July 1961:

' "Met a bod from Bradford called Richard Whiteley."

'I phoned Richard to tell him and he immediately asked, "What else did it say?" – presumably expecting me to announce "gorgeous, handsome, sexy". Sadly, to his everlasting mortification, nothing else was added and, had he not had such a superb memory for dates and places, I would never have realised that I had once spent an evening with this rather gauche young man who was to make such a mark on all our lives. At his 60th birthday party Richard announced in his speech that the 'first girl he had ever kissed' was present. I think this was a pretty apocryphal story, because we were rather late starters on the romantic front and I think a quick peck goodbye at the end of the evening after we had mooched hand in hand round the school block was all that happened!'

Although in Yorkshire Richard was happy to take girls out on dates and attend parties, he had still not broken up with Emma in London. So in the summer of that year, 1968, he went on holiday with her. They were joined by his new friend, Liz Fox from *Calendar* and two old friends, James Wilkinson and Iain Johnstone, who remembered that trip to Majorca with a grimace.

'I don't know which of us had chosen Magaluf,' reveals Iain. 'I suspect it was Emma; she usually made the decisions – but it was the most awful place imaginable, full of fish and chips and kiss-me-quick hats. I think the locals had designed it to please the British and knowing that we were shipped there in cramped charter flights with our knees touching our chins, they had covered the beach in row upon row of plastic chairs pressed up against each other.

'We spent the first days in the apartment reading books. Richard had brought *Jane Eyre* and would come to breakfast saying things like: "You're never going to believe this – Rochester is already married to this mad woman." And the response was "yes, yes, we believe it" because everybody else had read the book except for the Cambridge MA in English who appeared not to have opened that many novels while he was there.

'Things improved a bit when we hired a car and visited places like Deya where Robert Graves was still living. (We didn't see him.) There was a good deal of dry humour from James and Richard on those journeys. We drove over the brow of a hill to witness the most glorious expanse of Mediterranean in the setting sun. "The first person to see the sea has to pay a pound," James announced. There was a prolonged silence eventually broken by Richard: "Look at that big motorway down there." Silly stuff. I took up with a Finnish girl called Pirkko with whom there was a bit of a communication problem, my Finnish being as fluent as her English, and Richard creased himself with laughter when she unexpectedly turned up to live with me in London the next month.'

Returning home, Richard found it hard to sustain a long-distance relationship with Emma and things finally came to an end when he went to Julie Shaw's 21st birthday party in Huddersfield and met Jennie Greenwood. She was a small, bubbly blonde with a deep, sexy voice and Richard was immediately stricken. She shared a flat with a girl called Maggie Jackson who became a great friend of Richard's and Helen's and remains a stalwart friend of mine to this day.

Richard and Jennie went out for more than a year despite an early mishap when James Wilkinson had come to stay with him and they took Jennie and Julie out to dinner. Richard was by now the owner of his spanking new Triumph Vitesse. Having had a little too much wine with his meal he handed the keys to Jennie, who had had only a little less, to drive them back home across the Dales. Unfortunately she drove into a ditch and turned the car upside down. Miraculously, considering seat belts would not be made compulsory for another dozen years, they were shaken but not injured. When Jennie was breathalysed, she was found to be just under the limit. Julie recalled that Richard was so fond of Jennie that he never reproached her for the accident. 'He just said he was happy that we were all alive and simply got the car repaired.'

In late 1971 Richard began to feel curiously lethargic and, usually a healthy eater, lost his appetite. His skin began to go yellow and then the pigments of his eyes. Jaundice. Luckily his mum was there to look after him but he spent two months in bed before he was able to go back to work.

Many of YTV's staff were from London and discovered that one of the benefits of working in Leeds was that you could live in the countryside and drive into work in forty minutes or so.

While Richard was ill he had plenty of time for thought and, after he began to get his strength back, started to mark villages on a map of Yorkshire where he might look for a place of his own.

For a *Calendar* report he had gone to Masham and was greatly attracted to the market town and its beautiful square. The TV item was on how the famous real ale, Theakston Old Peculier Beer, got its name. The first part was easy: Robert Theakston founded the brewery in a hotel in Silver Street in 1827. But the Peculier was not so obvious. Masham was given to the Minster of York in the medieval period but, as the Archbishop did not wish to make the long journey north to oversee the town's affairs, the parish was designated a Peculier. This meant it had its own ecclesiastical court and governed its own affairs. To this day, the Vicar cannot be ordered to attend the Archbishop of York but must be formally invited.

Richard had met and liked Paul and Sue Theakston when he was filming the report and went back to see them when he got better. As he looked for properties, he found that there was nothing within his price range actually in Masham but rather in nearby Fearby Cross. An old lady had died and her executors were selling her cottage. It was at the end of a short terrace with, appealingly, a pub at the other end. The two-bedroom cottage, with its large garden, was just right for a bachelor and Richard negotiated down the price a bit – it only cost him three or four thousand pounds – and did the deal.

Iain Johnstone came up from London to celebrate Richard's first weekend in his new home and was amazed by Richard's hitherto unrevealed domesticity. He assumed Jennie must have done it but, no, that relationship was crumbling and Richard had fitted out the place with beds, chairs, a kitchen table and a fridge absolutely on his own. His mother had given him some of her old crockery and kitchenware. He had taken the week off to paint the walls and oversee the refitting of the kitchen. Iain gave him a wooden walking stick as a symbol of the country pleasures that lay in store and it still leans against our fireplace in The Parsonage.

When Richard considered the place suitably habitable and the lawn neatly mown, he had a marquee erected in the garden and threw a Sunday party.

Since many of the staff at Yorkshire Television were southerners who managed to get lost in Leeds, the chances of them finding a remote country cottage were – well – remote. So, in the manner of film and television location shoots, Richard nailed little wooden arrows to trees at every relevant turning from the A1 to Fearby Cross with the cryptic letters 'RW' on them.

This attracted the attention of more people than the invited. Paul Ashford was a local boy who had been brought up in Masham by his grandparents, helping out at their garage – the only one in town. He was a little younger than Richard. Always game for something new to experience and seeing these signs, the locals assumed a film star must have bought a holiday home in Fearby. This provoked discussion in the pub as who it might be. Robert Wagner? Richard Widmark? Raquel Welch?

Yes, after the sixth – or was it the seventh? – pint Paul and his chums decided it must definitely be Raquel Welch. And she would undoubtedly want to meet the locals so that she could feel fully integrated in the Yorkshire community. Come Sunday four of them pulled on their smartest suits and, fortified by a few more pints at the White Lion, bearing a welcoming present of a case of Theakston's Old Peculier, made their way to the end house of the terrace and entered the marquee.

It was quite crowded but Raquel was nowhere to be seen. Neither was Robert, nor Richard. At least not the Richard they might have expected. But there was a woman from the village passing among the guests with a tray and they were happy to help themselves to refreshments.

After about five minutes a young man with thick glasses came up to Paul and, with considerable politeness, enquired: 'Who are you?'

Paul had had a few by then and replied, a little more stoutly: 'Well, who are you?'

'The host,' said Richard.

'Ah,' Paul was confused. 'Well, we're all local. I've lived here all my life. My name's Paul and I work in the garage, George is a sales man and Simon – well, Simon doesn't actually have a job at the moment. So what do you do?'

At this point the increasing smile on their new-found host's lips dropped to the floor.

'You don't know?' he asked. 'Don't you watch television?'

'Yes, yes,' the uninvited guests nodded enthusiastically.

'Well, I'm on *Calendar*. The local news. On Yorkshire Television. At six o'clock.'

There was a silence, broken by Simon. 'We don't get Yorkshire Television here. We may live in North Yorkshire but we have to watch Tyne-Tees from Newcastle.'

Richard seemed almost palpably relieved. 'That explains it.' He rubbed his hands together. 'So welcome. Do stay.'

Paul held out the case of beer. 'Thanks, Richard. And welcome to Masham.'

They became friends – the poor boy who had grown up in Masham and the Giggleswick, Cambridge, ITN and YTV star. What Richard admired and envied – he had a great capacity for envy – about Paul was his clear-thinking, money-making schemes. Decimal currency was about to be introduced and Paul had obtained a regional franchise for the best cash registers. A little later, when people expected to get food in pubs and landlords installed microwaves, Paul started a business delivering them ready-to-heat meals such as lasagne or shepherd's pie. Richard christened him Pub Pot Paul and the name has stuck. In recent years Paul has built up an antiques business by having an eye for a bargain on eBay.

So Dick would drink at the weekends with Paul and his friends while also accepting an invitation from the local landowner, Lady Swinton of Masham, to come for cocktails.

Richard thought it might be time to take up some country pursuits and learn to ride. He discovered that Graham Ironside from the office was taking lessons and decided to join him.

Graham recalls: 'At one stage he was attracted by the charms of a young lady whose natural habitat was North Yorkshire, on the back of a horse. The equestrian world was one he much admired but one from which he was excluded because he couldn't ride: indeed, he scarcely knew which end would bite and which end would kick.

'Possibly dazzled by the seemingly effortless grace of John Whittaker and Robert Smith at the Horse of the Year Show, he determined he would impress his target after a few riding lessons.

'It was with more than a little misgiving that I introduced him to the equestrian disciplinarian who was trying to teach me to ride and we started lessons together anonymously and in privacy. As we thought.

'A couple of times a week, we would present ourselves for this unique form of physical and mental torture, rigid with fear but relentlessly driven on by pride. Hour after hour, we would pad around the riding school, wincing under a barrage of orders, few of which we could understand, far less attempt.

' "Keep your heels *down*." We could hardly keep our breakfast down.

' "Rise to the trot!" Rise?! We were bouncing up and down like pingpong balls.

' "Keep contact with the mouth." Good idea. We were already clinging on with everything else.

'Endlessly patient, the instructor went through her routines, second nature to any little girl old enough to climb into a pair of jodhpurs.

' "The pony won't know what to do if you don't apply the aids, chaps." Actually, the only reason we were able to carry on was exactly the opposite, thank goodness. The ponies knew exactly what to do and handled us with far more care than we handled them.

'We stuck doggedly to the task for several weeks, although we were beginning to accept that we were never likely to ride out with the York and Ainsty Hunt. The end came abruptly, one sunlit afternoon, when we – at last – realised we were not alone . . .

'Somewhere nearby, from behind the hedge, came the sounds of stifled giggles. They'd be silenced momentarily by whispered "Shsh's", only to break out anew, even louder. The culprits were those teenybopper pony-worshippers who seem to swarm round riding stables like midges in summer, enjoying some royal entertainment.

'Somehow the news had got around that Richard "Himoff Telly" was having riding lessons, a spectacle just too good to miss. And no doubt it was. Richard was not a natural rider. He bounced around like a sack of potatoes, his riding hat toppling this way and that, swaying dangerously from side to side, desperately embracing his mount round the neck every time it stopped.

'Thus his ardour for riding dissolved, and, funnily enough, so too, his ardour for the horsewoman of North Yorkshire. The bruising to his pride and the bruising to his backside disappeared almost as quickly.'

Around this time, Richard's sister, Helen, had been going out with a young barrister, James Stewart, who came from one of the most prominent Bradford families, a dynasty of doctors. His father, Henry Stewart, had been made a Freeman of the City the year before J.B. Priestley; he was an eminent surgeon and James's elder brother, Peter, was well on his way to becoming one. The oldest Stewart brother, John, was already a property millionaire.

James's first meeting with Richard was not auspicious. Very much the worse for wear, he escorted Helen home to Greencliffe Avenue where Kenneth Whiteley had just had a new drive laid. James got out of the car and vomited over it. Before he could be introduced to his future brother-in-law, later His Honour Judge Stewart, QC, Richard had to get out the hose and wash away his sick. After that, they got on very well.

Not to be outdone by his little sister, eighteen months later Richard himself got engaged to a very pretty interior designer, Candy Watson, whom he had met in Harrogate. She, too, was the daughter of a surgeon. They had a formal wedding at the church of St Mary Magdalene in

East Keswick. Iain Johnstone, the best man, had stayed the night in the Dragonara Hotel in Leeds and when he arrived at the church, which was more than half an hour away, realised to his horror that the wedding ring was still in the Dragonara Hotel. There was no other option but to use the wedding ring of his wife, Renate. When Candy, standing at the altar, saw this, a palpable shiver went through her body. Maybe she knew the marriage was doomed.

But they walked, smiling in the sun, from the church to her parents' garden for the reception. I know this because they showed the walk on *Calendar* the next Monday. They got married on 6 June 1973. I remember this well because it was three days after my 13th birthday. Richard meanwhile was just a few months short of his 30th birthday which was on 28 December of that year.

The memories that many people carry away from that afternoon was that there was a barrel-organ playing in the garden, Iain in his speech joked how Richard tried to bribe the vicar to cut the 'forsaking all others' out of the marriage oath and Mrs Watson spent much of the afternoon washing up paper plates and drying them in the oven. The more generous interpretation of this was that she had not seen a paper plate before.

Richard and Candy went to Minorca for their honeymoon which began on a boat and rapidly moved to dry land. Helen, by now, had had her first daughter, Alex, and insisted that Candy be one of the godmothers. The family all recall that the vicar on that occasion had eyes like Marty Feldman that pointed in different directions. They only came into sharp focus when Candy held her goddaughter next to her ample and not over-clothed bosom.

'When Candy used to come into the bar after the *Calendar* nightly news programme,' Richard later told *The Times*, 'the whole bar would stop and look at her. She had blonde curly hair, a lovely figure and people couldn't believe that an ugly bugger like me could get her. I don't know what she saw in me. But I was driving a Triumph Vitesse convertible at the time.'

Candy and Richard moved into his flat in Leeds – Woodlea Court. However well things went at first, they didn't subsequently. Eight months later Candy met another man and moved out. Richard came home to find a note of apology and a small amount of coffee for his breakfast. He was devastated and wore a black tie on *Calendar* for a whole year. But nobody noticed.

Richard sought solace with his sister and her husband, James. 'I think he bought Candy a car and that was that,' said his brother-in-law. 'He never really talked to me about it but I think he was very emotionally clipped – damaged.'

And Helen returned to her role as surrogate wife, chastising him for drinking too much, being too fat, for having dirty shoes and his lazy habit of cleaning them on the back of his trousers. Later if she ever heard he had been in the wrong place with the wrong girl, he would get a wigging for that as well. Richard rather liked it.

But tragedy hit the Whiteley (and Stewart) family for the first time. Alex had not been well and James was talking to a specialist in the Hermit pub about her symptoms – she had abdominal pains and could not put on weight. He urged the lawyer to have her tested for cystic fibrosis and the diagnosis, tragically, turned out to be positive. There was no cure; it meant she would not live to be 30. Her sister, Georgie, had just been born and they were terrified that she, too, would be affected. The odds of both parents being carriers were enormous. But Georgie was OK.

Helen and James resolved to be positive for Alex, not to tell her or anyone outside the family about her condition. They hoped that a cure might be found. Richard knew, and it drew the family much closer together with the Stewarts spending the weekends with him in Fearby, playing in the garden and going to Sunday morning service at St Mary's Church in Masham.

James's property-mogul brother had a flat in Filey where they took the girls in the summer. Richard would join them for weekends, reliving the days of his own childhood, picnicking on the beach and exploring the rock pools.

The weather in Filey was frequently less than clement; in fact there was a sea mist over the Brigg, known locally as the 'Filey Fret', which would linger all day if there was no sun strong enough to dissipate it.

This did little to spoil the fun of James Stewart or his brother Peter or their fellow father Duncan Feather. Indeed it provided them with an excuse to repair to the bar at Victoria Court on the Crescent. It was there that James got talking to an attractive blonde girl and her mother. She was called Caroline Barley and it turned out she worked as a physiotherapist at St James's Hospital in Leeds where Peter was a consultant urologist.

James invited Caroline to have dinner with him and Helen and Richard when he came up on Saturday night. Richard was greatly entranced with Caroline; she less so with him.

So he set about an elaborate courtship, not of her but her mother. Mrs Barley lived in Filey and owned a colourful beach hut on the shore. She liked to sit there and watch the sunset (when there was one) and Richard would invite himself along with a bottle of British Sherry – Mrs Barley's favourite tipple – and together they would put the woes of the world to rights.

It worked. Caroline – or Charley Barley as Dick rechristened her – became his first girlfriend since his divorce and they spent eighteen largely happy months together.

Until along came Jeni.

TEN

When you think of famous professional couples – Fred Astaire and Ginger Rogers, Bonnie and Clyde, Torvill and Dean, Fred and Wilma – if you live in the UK, you have to put Richard and Carol somewhere on your list. They were both involved in relationships with other people but, for viewers, their on-screen romance was warm and witty and cheering. As it was in real life. So how did it come about?

Well, *Countdown* was born in France. The talented producer, Armand Jammot, thought he would capitalise on the country's fondness for crosswords, numbers and pretentiousness by inventing a television show called *Des Chiffres et Des Lettres*. It was an immense success, played very seriously and getting up to 18 million viewers.

Frank Smith, a former Editor of *Panorama*, who had joined YTV as Head of Current Affairs, was a committed Francophile – he spoke several languages fluently including French and Russian – and spent much of his time in France. He thought the show would translate well to the British market.

So too, unfortunately, did an executive from Southern Television in Southampton who beat him to the draw. Unfortunately for them, Southern lost its franchise in the next lot of bids for ITV regions and thus had no station to play it on.

So Frank brought it to ITV and plucked a creative *Calendar* producer, John Meade, out of the rota to make a pilot. Sadly both men died relatively young, but not before they had knocked the programme into British shape. Frank decided that there should be a clock in the centre of the set – there isn't one in the French game – and John decided that they would have more letter games than number games – they are 50–50 in France – because, he said, 'the Brits were less numerate than the Frogs'.

There was unanimity on who would present this series of six regional shows called *Calendar Countdown* – the main regional front man, of course. They felt the need for a celebrity and the flavour of the time was Ted Moult, a farmer from Ticknall in Derbyshire, who had risen to fame on the BBC's *Any Questions* and *Ask Me Another*. He looked like a farmer, spoke like a farmer but had a sharp, knowledgeable brain. He, too, is no longer with us, having committed suicide in 1986 at the age of 60.

To round out the cast there was a lexicographer from Leeds University in Dictionary Corner, pretty Cathy Hutner who was not allowed to speak but whose job was to put up the letters and numbers, and Denise McFarland-Smith who had both brains and beauty and was attired in academic dress to emphasise her IQ of 168.

The shows were recorded and the first one was transmitted at 6.30 p.m. on Monday, 6 July 1982. The studio audience seemed to like the programmes, judging by their response, and later they discovered so did the viewing public: the ratings were tremendous.

So Frank Smith took the best programme down to Channel 4 in London to show to Cecil Korer, the Commissioning Editor for Light Entertainment. He liked it and said he would have fifty of them. Cecil seemed to think Cathy's task was too arduous so he suggested the job be split with a former Miss

United Kingdom, Beverly Isherwood, putting up the numbers. Mental arithmetic had not proved Denise McFarland-Smith's forte (she went on to become a highly-paid intellectual property lawyer) so the hunt was on for a presentable girl who could do her sums.

Compared with Richard, Carol Vorderman had a tough upbringing. 'I was born in Bedford. My father was Dutch. He worked with the Resistance and came over during the war. But my parents separated when I was 3 weeks old and my mother moved to North Wales which was where she was from. So she had me, 3 weeks, my brother aged 8 who had a severe cleft lip and palate – he's had 23 or 24 operations – and my sister who was then 10. My brother couldn't speak by the age of 8 and my mother had absolutely no money. But my uncle had a house and he let her rent the downstairs flat of this house for a pound a week. My mother had four part-time jobs which she had to keep doing because there was no child support agency, no child benefit or anything like that. You just had to do what you had to do.

'I have always loved numbers. At the age of 3 or 4 I was way ahead of my class so I was put to one side. The teacher said "Do these pluses and minuses, do as many as you can". So I just raced through them. At the age of 4 or 5 I was doing the work of kids two years older than I was. So they put me up a year and that's where I stayed. I went to Cambridge from a Catholic comprehensive school when I was 17.

Getting onto *Countdown* involved a huge sequence of happy coincidences, so much so I would come to regard it as fate. I was 20 when I graduated and got a job selling computers. I was crap at it. I could never do as a salesman says "the close" – close the deal – because I thought "Well, it's up to you really; if you want to buy it, that's fine." My mother had divorced my stepfather and was living in digs in Windsor and I had a boyfriend in Leeds whom I used to visit. And I said to my mother: "Houses are ever so cheap there and you're paying rent. A house in Yorkshire, you'll love it." She had never been to Yorkshire in her life. But she said, "Yes, darling that's fine." So when I was 21 I organized this joint mortgage; my brother, who was doing well in Europe, gave us a deposit.

'That was in July 1982. Just three weeks later there was an article in the *Yorkshire Evening Post*. *Calendar Countdown* had gone out and now it had been commissioned by Channel 4. They wanted to make it in the September and the article said that the girl who had done my job in the pilot series of six was leaving to go to university. I can remember reading it, thinking: "What does she want to leave a job like that for to go to university?" Without telling me my mother, Jean, wrote this letter, including my graduation photograph, and forged my signature.

'I got a letter asking me to come for an interview. I thought, "Oh, it's a bit of a lark. I'll go down but of course I won't be on the telly. Don't be ridiculous." Women on the telly were either Angela Rippon, Esther Rantzen, Anna Ford, or they were dolly dealers. You were one or the other. I think it was only five years previously that the very first female newsreader was on. At that time everyone on the telly was a star because there were only three channels. There was no breakfast television, no reality television. There was BBC1, BBC2 and ITV and that was your lot and there was no daytime television. So any newsreader was a huge star. Everybody knew them. It didn't matter who you were, if you were on the telly you were in an unattainable stratosphere really. Not like it is today at all where everyone thinks, "Oh, I can do that, it's easy."

'The producer John Meade was an eccentric Yorkshireman who just told me what the rules were although, strictly speaking, arithmetically, his explanation was wrong. He showed me a mute recording of the French programme and stopped the tape and said, "Right, this is what they've got. These are the numbers. Right do it." I did it very, very quickly and I got them all right. I think he was relieved to have actually found someone. In fact the reason they couldn't find anyone was because he hadn't explained the thing right in the first place. John said, "That's great, you'll have to come back for a screen test." He seemed impressed by how quickly I could do the sums. He told me there had been this bloke in who had written 40 books about statistics and he wasn't very good at it – he couldn't do a thing. They had put adverts in the *Guardian*, all the national papers and they couldn't find anybody. He couldn't believe that I lived two miles up the road in Headingley. I could do it and I was young. That was it – I got the job!.

'I met Richard and he was charming but I didn't have any contact with him on air; I just worked out the numbers. He was desperately trying to be serious. His persona in those days was so different to what it became. So different. In those days Richard would present it with a very knowing, "yes I am so intelligent, I am a newscaster, don't you know". He wasn't the Richard who we came to love at all. Twenty-three years ago he was quite pompous as I often told him. But I didn't dare tell him that then. In fact, I didn't really have a lot to do with him because, of course, he was the big star and I was just a little thing. He introduced me on the first show: "We have this very intelligent young lady, she will be here to answer the numbers game. She is known as our vital statistician, ha, ha, ha, Carol Vorderman." And I sort of looked at the floor and muttered: "Hello?"

'The only thing that worried me was, was I going to get it right? So while all the letters games were going on I would be practising. I would write out my own numbers games giving myself targets. I have pages where I will write out six numbers, including one or two from the top. Then I will go down and I will write targets – three lots of targets for each set and while the clock is going round I will try and do four of them in each clock. So it just gets your brain going in the right way. I get it spot on in the time, even now 90 per cent of the time, and that is good enough.

'The big joke was that Richard was useless at arithmetic and that is the truth. But very occasionally, if I didn't get it exactly right, he would be told down his earpiece and pretend he had, little monkey. I never wore an earpiece. Michael Wylie in the control room is very good at maths, because he had been a bookie in the days before computers. Michael and I still fight each other on the numbers. So if I don't get a number, even now I say to Lisa the floor manager: "Did Michael get it?" She has to whisper into her mike: "Did Michael get the numbers game then?" And obviously he will always say yes, but then Lisa says he didn't really. There is a lot of joshing going on. It's a constant on *Countdown,* which is lovely. It's part and parcel of what it is.

'In the early days I used to irritate Richard a lot because I have always loved messing around with the props boys and chatting. Unfortunately, I didn't realise what eyelines were in those days. I was more or less in Richard's eyeline for his camera, in other words, just behind his camera so if he was talking he could just see me in the corner of his vision. It used to really annoy him and he used to tell me off a lot in the bar after the show. "Stop talking when I am trying to record." It didn't strike me at the time but he was right. Then I used to do it a little bit deliberately to aggravate him.

'I will never ever forget the first time I mentioned his jackets on air. I mean, they were, in those days, utterly vile jackets. He had genuinely bad taste. I remember saying something to him around 1985. Richard, because he was quite formal in those days, was always so intelligent and all gushing, which was very nice because he was being very polite, and then I flung the first insult which was something about his jackets. I said: "Richard, how can you wear that jacket?" And it took him by surprise. It was a screaming sort of yellow and red stripes, I mean it was just revolting with a checked shirt and a spotted tie – just appalling. He said: "Don't ever say that to me again. I am the Quizmaster of this show blah blah." And he really went for it in private later. He was not happy about it. I don't think anybody had commented about his dress sense before.

Richard was very supportive of me. He was an important figure in Yorkshire Television, and YTV was an important television company. Richard knew all of the bosses and owners very well indeed. After a year on *Countdown* I decided to give up my full-time job of selling computers and try my hand in telly full-time. Richard had a brainwave. He asked the then boss of all the local programmes, including *Calendar* if he would consider me as a weather girl! He hadn't asked me about it but he thought it was a good idea because I was good at standing next to a board (the numbers board) waving my arms around. Graham Ironside, the boss, thought the idea was one of the most ridiculous he'd ever heard and said to Whiters: "I've seen that wee lassie on *Countdown* Richard, and I'm telling you now that she has no future in television." Richard loved to tell that tale, particularly in later years when I was all over every channel.

'Another reason why I loved Richard was that he could tell the same story over and over again and still laugh at it, and make me laugh too. Whenever I was feeling a bit low or fed up about something I knew that I could nip down to his dressing room and ask him to tell me a favourite story. I could listen to his stories endlessly and he always made me feel better. Others would say: 'But he's told you that story thirty times before' and they didn't understand that it was our way of being together. I didn't care how often he'd told it before, in fact the more he'd told it, the more I loved it. We had a shorthand, the more he said a particular phrase on *Count-down* the more I laughed, I just couldn't tire of him because he would laugh too.

'There had been various girls doing the letters after Cathy Hutner left, including lovely Karen Loughlin who went on to marry football manager Graham Souness; the last one re-signed because she said she wanted to be known as an actress not a television hostess, which seemed fair enough. We were due back on air in the April so at our very drunken Christmas lunch which happened every year, which would always end up with Rick Vanes (the scriptwriter), John Meade, me and Whiters, Meade started saying something which I deciphered as being along the lines of, "Do you think you're too fucking good to do the letters?" laughing away. So I said, "No I don't, I can do letters, hic hic." And he said, "Alright, Vorders, you're on." So that was basically how I came to do the letters. Then Meade realised once he had sobered up weeks later that he had also saved himself money. He didn't increase my fee by a single penny so from just answering the numbers I went to do the whole thing and that was when Richard and I really started working together. Because previously I was only on for two lots of 45 seconds.

'I had moved down to London and Richard came down when he was doing *Calendar* for political things, but then he gave *Calendar* up and he used to come down socially and I enjoyed those days because by then he had become more and more immature as the years went on and I had grown up into my proper age and he had come down with his age so we were actually well matched by that time. He always called me "little one". When we would walk to the studio together along the corridor he'd say "Come on, little one" and hold my hand. He only had little hands. We'd wander down the corridor and then amble into the studio and the audience would burst into applause. I noticed how our lovely *Countdown*ers (that's the official term for people who watch *Countdown*) loved him more as the years went on. You could tell by how they were with him and what they said about him. In the first ten years, I'd often be asked, "What's that Richard Whiteley really like? Is he as much of a pillock as he looks on the telly?" And so on. But then as the years progressed and our ratings went through the roof, the questions and comments changed. "Oh, I love that Richard. Is he as funny as he is on the telly? My Mum adores him." And the students would wear strange ties in his honour and worship him as their daft loveable uncle. He basked in it. It was all so beautifully innocent. He loved *Countdown*. I loved *Countdown*. Our audience loved *Countdown*, and eventually even the bosses came to like it too.

'Richard and I were convinced that *Countdown* was a bit of an embarrassment to Channel 4, in spite of its huge ratings. We were getting nearly 5 million viewers a day and many weeks for about 10 years we owned the top 5 places in the Channel 4 top 10. The list would read 1 *Countdown* (Monday) 2 *Countdown* (Tuesday) 3 *Countdown* (Friday) 4 *Countdown* (Thursday) 5 *Countdown* (Wednesday) and then there'd be some other shows. But *Countdown* wasn't cool so we were largely ignored by the press and important people in telly. Richard would often make up a story about how our boss would react to the ratings that week. He'd make up situations where the then boss, Michael Grade (now chairman of the governors at the BBC), would be asked which was the top-rated show on his vibrant progressive youthful Channel at some international TV conference, and he'd have to admit that it was us. Richard would say, "And then Michael Grade would have to say, well it's a little quiz show called *Countdown*' and then I'd cheer and we'd both end up in curled up with laughter. We always knew what *Countdown* was. It was a little parlour game with no big money prizes, with not very funny jokes, no script and a bunch of letters stuck on pieces of lino which an ageing bird (that's me) would put on a wooden board and then a clock would go round for 30 seconds where nothing televisually would happen. Then the host (that's him) would get the contestants' names wrong, wear something hideous and laugh at his own lines. Someone would win and no money was ever handed out. Big London media types didn't particularly like it but we revelled in it. We were often treated with scorn in the press but it never bothered us. The only time we would get angry, and I mean furious, is if anyone ever criticised our audience. As far as we were concerned, we (and that means all *Countdown*ers as well) were in this together for the long term. *Countdown*ers are the people who kept the show going for decades and we knew just how lucky we were – and believe me we were exceptionally grateful.

Richard was always getting into trouble unwittingly. One Christmas a *Countdown*er had sent in a hand-painted silk tie with the word COUNTDOWN painted vertically down the front. It was tastefully done, so Richard wore it on a Christmas show. We recorded the whole show, all went home, thought nothing more about it until it was broadcast. He'd made the front pages, this time because he'd been sitting through the entire show with the DOWN part of the word hidden behind the desk and his microphone covering the letter O in COUNT. You can imagine the trouble. Hilarious and innocent.

'One of the many wonderful qualities of Whiteley is that in many ways he was completely unpredictable – whenever we went out we never quite knew what time we'd get back or where we'd end up. He had a penchant for mischief. Here's just one example.

'About half past eleven one morning, I was filming in London and my mobile phone rang. It was Whiters. "Darling, where are you, are you free for lunch?" Well, as it happened I was finishing work early so I was free. "Come to the Sloane Club, darling, and we'll have something to eat, we can have a little chat." So I went to the Sloane Club. "Vorders, You must meet this great girl." And he introduced me to some lady in her 60s. Everyone was a "great girl" to Richard which was charming. He never saw people cynically, everyone was marvellous and more beautiful in his world. Anyway, we started at the Sloane Club about noon, followed by lunch across the road in a great Italian restaurant at 2 p.m. We were poured out of there about half past six and went to some drinks party he knew was happening. That ended early about 9 p.m., so we went to a drinks reception at Channel 5 for Dawn Airey's fantastic assistant Elspeth who had just received her MBE. It was now about 11 p.m. and we didn't want to go home. A friend of mine said she was going to Joe Allen's (the late night restaurant in Covent Garden), so somehow we managed to stumble our way there. Then she had brought a good friend of hers along, Bianca Jagger.

Now Bianca Jagger is an exceptionally sophisticated person who is known as one of the most elegant ladies in the world. So Richard plonked himself next to her with his stripey jacket and for the next two hours made her laugh so much, as he tried to persuade her that she needed "more meat on her bones so let's start with sausage and mash". He was hysterical. Our "lunch" ended fourteen hours later at about 2.30 a.m. with me standing on Drury Lane waving goodbye to him tucked up in the back seat of a Honda Civic laughing away innocently with Bianca Jagger. There has only ever been one Richard Whiteley.

'It's funny, isn't it, until somebody is gone you don't analyse what you think about them. Whiters was always there. He was my continuity really during my happiest times. I'm not saying I wasn't happy when I was a child, but he was always there as this rock. He changed over the years a lot. I would say the last five years were the happiest. He just relaxed into himself.'

Carol was just devastated by Richard's death. She had lost her professional partner and she knew things would never be the same again.

Richard was not the perfect host for everyone. Eighteen months into the run of *Countdown* the suits at Channel 4 under Jeremy Isaacs decided they liked the show but felt it might be more popular with a more famous host. Someone like Bob Monkhouse. Richard and John Meade set off for Monte Carlo for the grand final of *Des Chiffres et Des Lettres* and a gala dinner in the presence of Prince Rainier and his family.

In *Hamlet*, you will recall, King Claudius tells Rosencrantz and Guildenstern to accompany Hamlet to England, with a secret plan to get rid of him. In similar fashion Paul Fox and John Fairley told John Meade that he was to inform Richard that he was being replaced as host of *Countdown*, but only after he had enjoyed the delights of Monte Carlo. Fortunately Dick was saved by the ratings. While they were away it emerged that *Countdown* editions had got into the Channel 4 top ten. Fox faxed Meade at his Monaco hotel to say that the plan had been abandoned. Richard subsequently found out about it and, since he didn't have a mean bone in his body, never held it against Fox and Fairley with whom he remained friendly until he died.

Richard was finding the workload of 15 *Countdown*s and 5 *Calendar*s a week stressful. They could always start again when he welcomed *Countdown* viewers to '*Calendar*' but not when he welcomed *Calendar* viewers to '*Countdown*' as the programme was live. He felt unable to share the problem with anyone at YTV so he discussed it with his old colleague, Bob Warman.

'We were at Henley Regatta, in the car park where Peter and Christine Stewart entertained,' Bob recalls. 'I wandered over to find them and there was this great party going on. Ricco grabbed hold of me, saying we had to talk. He looked a bit desperate. We wandered off over the cricket pitch and sat in the pavilion to ruminate over various things. He announced that he was going to make what was for him a very big decision: he was going to leave *Calendar*. I said: "Think about that carefully because *Calendar* is the one thing that is consistent. It will always be there."

'*Countdown* was getting good viewing figures and I guess he just found the pressure maybe too much to do the two of them together. Also, I think *Calendar* had adopted a new style which, perhaps, wasn't his. It wasn't his programme any more because *Calendar* was always very much the Richard Whiteley programme really, *Richard Whiteley at Six,* and the style had changed as it had for a lot of these regional programmes. I don't think he liked the way it was going particularly and he just saw a greater future in *Countdown*. But I have to say I was very concerned for him at that time. I thought that it was a risky move because, although *Countdown* has lasted all these years subsequently, it was never on the cards that it was going to go on for ever and ever, as it turned out. But he seemed fairly determined that that was what he was going to do. And it certainly did.'

In 1993, John Willis, no longer the young researcher Richard had befriended on *Calendar,* became Director of Programmes at Channel 4 and there was a distinctly different attitude to Richard and the programme, as John recalls.

'I inherited *Countdown* and championed it. It was getting four-plus million viewers. We looked at new ways of revamping daytime but I always thought that *Countdown* was the heart of the daytime schedule. It had lots of loyal viewers; it seemed to attract both students and old ladies at the same time, which is a fantastically unusual and clever trick. We built the schedule around it. It used to run for half the year but I turned it into a 52 week-a-year series. Richard always said that *that* was the thing that actually transformed *Countdown* and turned him into a major celebrity. Because it was always doing very well but it became much more habitual and

Richard, of course, was on television nearly every day of the year, except weekends.'

As they grew older, Richard and John Willis began to look more and more like each other, much to the latter's amusement. 'It's a tragic indictment of my dietary regime that I was mistaken for him on lots of different occasions. The first time was at Yorkshire Television. There was a coach-load of snowy-haired *Countdown* fanatics who had come from Bridlington and they were queuing up in the corridor outside the studio. As I walked along, one of them got excited and said: "Here he is!" And they all assumed I was Richard. I didn't know what to do. And they all got their autograph books out and shouted: "Sign your autograph, Richard." I sort of protested, "I'm not Richard," and they just laughed. There were about thirty or forty of them so I just started signing their autograph books, you know: "To Gladys, love Richard", "To Mabel, love Richard" and they were all extremely satisfied.'

'Many years later, when I was at Channel 4, I took Richard and Bill Stewart from *Fifteen to One* to the races at Cheltenham which Channel 4 used to carry. We were all in a carriage together. But when I left it and walked up the corridor to the gents, people hummed the *Countdown* tune at me. Later in the day, I was going down to the race track just with Bill Stewart and one of the waitresses who was serving food there came up to me and said: "Oh, Richard, can I have your autograph?" And Bill said: "He's not Richard but I'm Bill Stewart, the real Bill Stewart from *Fifteen to One*." And she said: "I don't like *Fifteen to One*, I'm only interested in him and *Countdown*." And Bill said: "He's not him. The real Richard is in the box back there." She said: "Don't try and pull my leg, this is Richard."

'Once it actually happened the other way round, which did give me a great deal of satisfaction. It was at a rather formal Independent Television Commission Christmas party. Richard was already there and talking to some senior ITC executives and I arrived in time to hear one of them say to him: "Well done, John, on the Channel 4 censorship season." They then saw me and became completely perplexed that there were two Richards – or two Johns, in this instance.'

Christa Ackroyd recalled Richard's latterday pressures. 'He was nervous before every programme, going through scripts because I don't think he had ever read them. He was always two minutes late for everything, always playing catch-up. He once actually missed the start of *Calendar*. I stood in the newsroom where we were supposed to be doing the opening and they said: "Where's Richard, where's Richard?" I said: "I don't know, I am not his keeper. I don't know where he is." So they sent people out looking here, there and everywhere. We were live on air and I went: "Good evening and welcome to *Calendar*." He should have been there so they quickly tightened the shot, and the door opened behind me in the newsroom and in wandered Richard. Everybody said to him: "Where the hell have you been? You've been doing this programme for 20 years and it has always started at the same time." He turned round and said to the female producer: "You mustn't blame yourself, it is completely my fault," and she said: "We know." Do you know where he was? He was watching a *Countdown* tape. He had missed the broadcast the day before.'

Which was only too true. In all the time I lived with him, Richard never missed a *Countdown* transmission, whether live or taped on VHS. It had been recorded weeks before so he could come to it fresh, laughing at the jokes – including his own – and frequently failing to solve the Conundrum, although he had presided over it. He had an instinct that the programme should never change and if he kept an eye on it from a viewer's perspective, it never would.

It is well-nigh impossible for me to have an objective view of *Countdown*. I always enjoyed it and I loved the presenter! But from everything I have read about the programme by people who were not involved with it one piece stands out. Entitled: 'Why I Love My Cosy Half-Hours with Carol and Richard', it was written by the distinguished novelist and art critic, Philip Hensher, and published by the *Independent* in May 2001.

The idle freelancer quickly discovers that daytime television throws up some real curiosities, but none, surely, odder than *Countdown*. Most of the networks' daylight offerings I find barely watchable, despite serious application; those chatty sofa programmes practically reduce me to tears, so clearly do they imply the misery and boredom of their regular audience.

But the one absolutely shining, unmissable, programme of the day is Channel 4's incredible, unique *Countdown*. In my house, anyone who telephones between 4.30 and 5 p.m. on a weekday gets very short shrift indeed. The quiz is inconceivably addictive, and an object of unending fascination. It is no surprise at all that *Countdown* has just celebrated its 3,000th edition, or that it features almost every week in the top viewing figures of the channel. It's been going for 20 years now, and to be honest, I think there is no reason for it ever to finish.

The game is terribly simple. Two contestants ask for letters to be taken from two piles of vowels and consonants, until a nine-letter jumble is produced; they then have 30 seconds to produce the longest word they can. There are six rounds of that, and two of a numbers game, in which the contestants must multiply, divide, add and subtract six numbers to come as near as they can to a given total. That's it. The whole thing takes place on a set which might have hosted a game show in East Germany in 1976; there is no prize, but a 'goody-bag', comprising a dictionary, a T-shirt and a mug. There is a celebrity guest and a girl with a dictionary, Carol Vorderman simpering and Mr Richard Whiteley, a host of spectacular vagueness.

I've tried and tried to explain the incredible appeal of *Countdown*, without ever really succeeding. There are a few jokes that no one ever gets tired of, about Richard's wig and Wetwang, a village in Yorkshire which everyone joked about so much that in the end they elected Richard its mayor, Gipsy Creams, the cult status of Susie Dent, the demure girl with the dictionary, and the ongoing unrequited passion of Richard for Carol.

In part the appeal is the amazing, adorable ineptitude of the whole thing. Richard is quite capable of reading out a viewer's letter or poem, and then saying bluntly: 'I don't think that's very good, really.' He's been going through the same routine every day for 20 years and still loses his place – I treasure the memory of the day he went completely blank at the end and just said 'Well, that's all, so we'll just say goodbye now and leave you, er, with the credits' before staring at the camera for four seconds of silence.

In part, too, it's the suspicion that one day things will go terribly wrong; that a contestant will say 'Consonant, consonant, vowel, consonant' and Carol will produce the word TWAT. The appeal is slightly odd, since I have to admit to being no good at the game at all; it is a good round when I manage to find a five-letter word, and yet I absolutely adore the show.

Half an hour a day with a cup of tea, a plate of Gipsy Creams and listening to Richard and Carol bickering cosily in exactly the same way they were doing 10 years ago, and will be doing 10 years from now; half an hour a day watching people who are unmistakably happy to be doing what they do. Sheer joy: I hope it goes on, without the slightest alteration, forever.'

I wish.

ELEVEN

J eni Cropper played a substantial part in Richard's life. They lived together for more than a dozen years in the house he bought in Burley Woodhead. But, as she freely admits, there were other women around and indeed my friendship with Richard continued while he lived with Jeni. She came to his funeral and we talked about him.

Today Jeni lives nearby in Ilkley, still single and still the attractive and humorous girl who was Richard's companion for such a long time but whom he never married. She has a successful marketing business which she started on her own and her parents live nearby. Both of them are locals from Leeds. Her dad was a Group Captain in the RAF, serving on Lancaster Bombers during the Second World War.

Jeni was born in RAF Waddington, near Lincoln and, when she was seven, swapped the grey prefabs of the base for the white wastelands of Alaska where her father was posted. 'We lived in Elmendorf,' she recalls, 'just outside Anchorage. There was a base there. Alaska is very hot. It's very dry so when it's cold it's cold and you are not allowed to put your hands on metal otherwise you would stick to it.'

She and her sister went to a local school for service children. Although the family moved house more than thirty times, she was not so fortunate when her dad was sent to Gan, a staging post for aircraft and a luxurious holiday resort in the Maldive Islands in the Indian Ocean, with sandy beaches and turquoise lagoons. There was no accommodation for officers' families so her mother moved to North Yorkshire and Jeni and her sister went to Casterton boarding school. She hated it and, at night, she would hold hands with the girl in the next bed, Didy Metcalf. In the winter their hands became so cold they would cover them with a towel.

Jeni was always interested in business and, after obtaining her HND, she specialised in marketing and public relations. When the brand new franchise, Yorkshire Television, started recruiting in Leeds at the beginning of 1968, she could well have applied for a job had she not already got a good one. But many of her friends did and one of them was Carole Tudor, the first girl whom Richard 'kissed'.

Carole and Richard had become great friends and, when one or the other was short of a partner, would go to parties or even hunt balls together. Carole would even go to his house and do his ironing in return for lashings of red wine. Then Richard formed a more permanent relationship with Charley (Caroline Barley). It started to become fractious after eighteen months because she was very anxious to get married and he – once bitten very badly – wasn't. So they split up. Or seemed to split up.

Jeni recalls: 'It was at that time that Carole was very insistent on us getting together. I was fairly fancy free. Sort of in-between. And she decided this was the time. She said you are both my best friends – he is my best male friend and you are my best female friend so therefore you should be together. That was her reasoning. She arranged this meeting in a wine bar and I think Richard was late. Certainly we had met a few friends by the time he arrived and were having quite a good time and I think we had ordered and then the tornado came in, as in Charley. She just ran in, spotted him with lots of girls and went home to Buxton Hall in Alwoodley. Then she rang him to say she was upset, so he explained he had better go. He didn't rush; I think she had said such things before. I thought, well, this is not the man for me because he is obviously involved or he isn't quite the right person to be with, by which time I was being chatted up by someone else. We ate and then we left. But the bizarre thing is that after he'd checked Charley was okay, he apparently came back to the wine bar thinking we'd still all be there. In fact there were very few people there but he still finished his dinner.

'He called me after a few weeks and asked me out for a drink. I went, but I warned him that I was already in love so therefore couldn't fancy him. I had met an estate agent, also called Richard, and had fallen for him. I was in love at that time but it didn't last very long. He did ask me to marry him – the other Richard. But he smothered me and that must have finished, I suppose, in the November and I bumped into Richard at some point in Ilkley during the Christmas period. I was invited to a New Year's Eve party – 1980 turning into 1981 – and I asked him to come. He eventually arrived way into the evening and drove me home. It was the first and the last time he ever drove me.

'At the beginning of that January when I first met him I had gone on this allergy test diet because I had really bad arthritis, and no alcohol was allowed and I was coming off the diet but I still wasn't drinking. Richard's friends sort of interviewed me. They thought I was on a drying-out phase because I was an alcoholic – a source of great amusement later. He was living in Burley Woodhead and I was living in Burley in Wharfedale coincidentally. I had bought a house for £8,500 because Burley was cheaper than Ilkley. Richard and I didn't live together until 1984 and I sold that house. He liked me to be with him but he didn't really want me to be there all the time so that I was his responsibility. Richard would much rather have had everything and nothing. The day I confronted him about it, I think we went out for a long lunch and I sort of said, look, this is ridiculous, I am never at my home. I could rent it out and come and live with you, what about it? He said yes. I think Richard feared it would curtail his activities. It meant that he couldn't bring women home any more if I was there, so that debunked that, and also I just might know what he was doing all the time which turned out to be bollocks, actually, because he said he would never ever lie to me which meant, on occasion, he didn't talk to me a lot.

'I met Richard's mother and father fairly rapidly. We were walking along the Grove in Ilkley and they were driving past and they stopped. He was slightly embarrassed because I don't think he had told his father at that stage that we were living together and he invited them back for tea. His mother, Margaret, was lovely: very chummy and friendly and open-minded. Obviously she wanted to know who I was and that was alright. But his father wouldn't say very much, he would sort of pace around a bit and say, "Are you going to get this place sorted out or what? Why haven't you done this?" There was always a bit of tension between them. It wasn't always an easy relationship.

'Richard's sister, Helen, was married to James and they had their two daughters who idolised Richard. Helen was more down to earth. We got on very well but she was never a close friend. She was not of my sort, she didn't work – then anyway, she later went to work at the Yorkshire Clinic – she was a mother and her friends were mothers with kids.

'But she had an enormous influence on Richard. Both of them were enormous *Coronation Street* addicts. Richard never missed an episode – he would tape it if he was working. And when we were on holiday she would tape them for him and bring him up to date. But she used to bully him and tell him off. Richard's shoes were always dirty, those awful shoes he insisted on wearing – slip-on things which made his feet cold and look dreadful. I made him buy some beautiful black broguey ones but he never wore them. But he absolutely loved Helen and was very proud of her and her sparkiness and she would always find out the things that he didn't want her to find out. I could as well, but her even more so. She would say, "I hear you were drunk in the wine bar the other night?" "No

I wasn't." "Yes you were, you were there with so and so, so and so told me."

'Really my life with Richard revolved around weekends. I'd come back from wherever I had been on Friday, he would do the same thing, we'd probably have a Friday row as everybody does, go to the Hermit, the pub at the top of our lane in Burley, for a drink or go out for a meal. The Hermit was tiny and there was a small group of regulars, especially our neighbour, Keith Feather. The guy behind the bar, Bob, was extremely grumpy. I think he had been in textiles and fallen on hard times. He was okay with the regulars but tended to view the place as a private club. When any stranger came into the pub, everybody would be quiet, and they would have to walk past everybody being quiet and looking at them. They would fight their way to the bar for a drink and we wouldn't move. Then they would usually say: "Do you serve food?" and Bob would snap back: "Yes – salt and vinegar or unsalted."

'Then on Saturday we would drive up to the cottage in Fearby, which was only forty minutes away. It was more relaxing there, not least because they couldn't get *Calendar* – or *Countdown*, to begin with. We would always meet up with Pub Pot Paul and Chrissie (Paul's first wife) and Ray and various old friends. It was usually the pub or a party on Saturday night and then on Sunday either I or one of the girls would cook late lunch that would stretch into the evening. Happy days.

'Richard and I went to Egypt for his 40th birthday because he said he wanted to see the Valley of the Kings. (Actually we went to Egypt because he said if he went somewhere that was thousands of years old, 40 became insignificant!) I gave him a present every day of the holiday, so I didn't give him a big present, I gave him little presents. We did the Nile Cruise. We went up to one of the ancient tombs and always, on the way, there are locals selling things. I have to say Richard always bought something because he couldn't resist, he couldn't say no. This guy came up to us and said, "Lady, lady, please buy this silk scarf or something." Then he said, "Hello, Richard."

He was Egyptian but he was a student at Manchester University. It made Richard's day.

'Then there was the holiday we spent with Iain and his second wife, Mo, in Don Robinson's apartment in Fort Lauderdale in Florida. It seemed to be in a retirement complex and Mo was desperate for a tan but the sun barely shone for the first few days and an old resident advised her, "You've got to catch it when it's out." Richard and I flew up to Orlando to go to Disneyland and it was so cold there that we had to buy additional sweaters. The only ones you could get were bright yellow or pink with Goofy or Donald Duck emblazoned on them. We had to walk around in those.

'When we got back, we went for dinner in some posh restaurant in Palm Beach and the meal we ordered just wouldn't come. Richard dived into the wine which gave him the courage to summon the head waiter. And he informed him pompously, "There is something wrong in the kitchen. I know about these things as I happen to own a chain of restaurants in England." Which was news to the rest of us. But then the guy came back after about half an hour and admitted the chef had in fact walked out so we ended up at McDonalds.

'We would only go to the races because Yorkshire TV would sponsor a race and they would have a box, so I have never been to the races when I have not been in a box. And only YTV people would go. So I would say, "Why haven't you got any of your big advertisers here?" But there would just be us and that was it. Sometimes they used to ask people like the odd mayor, and one time it was a very cold day and as we walked from the car park to the box it started to snow. We got into the box and they had got one of those extra heaters, one of those calor gas things, and we were having our first glass of champagne and we could all smell this awful burning and the woman mayor was standing against it with her fur coat, and her fur coat had caught fire.

'So, all these corporate jobs including going to the likes of the Grosvenor in London for some dinner, or Royal Television Awards, there would just be us – Geoff Brownlee, John

Fairley, John Wilford, Richard and me and a few others. On the table would be six bottles of red, six bottles of white, a bottle of gin, a bottle of whisky, a bottle of brandy, port, whatever, and at the end of the night everybody used to take them home. The same at the races – there would be the bar completely stacked with stuff and everybody would just take whatever was left home.

'Richard had been on the screen in *Calendar* for more than a dozen years by this time so he did a lot of Public Appearances in the Yorkshire region. He loved doing them – he'd open anything, he'd go to anything, he'd be the guest speaker at anything, he'd be the guest at anything and so I was really dragged along. He liked it because he loved to get out and know as many of his public as he could. He did love the adulation. Things like speaking at the annual dinner of the Thurnscoe Harmonic Male Voice Choir which comes from a small mining village near Barnsley. I remember there was this classic time when we were on the top table at a dinner and I wasn't sitting next to him, and it took until the pudding course before my either side partner both said to me: "Actually, who are you?" We had a very nice conversation all through dinner but they had no idea who I was because Richard was never good at saying, "this is Jeni Cropper, she is with me blah de blah". Richard Whiteley and guest. It would drive me nuts and he would never get my name on the invitation. Presumably if I pulled out he could invite someone else.

'He was appointed a Governor of Giggleswick School in 1981. That came about through his very good friends Susan and Warwick Brookes. Warwick was deputy headmaster and they were looking for another Governor and Susan had suggested Richard, mainly because he was devoted to the school and would make a very good one. The other Governors obviously considered it and he was duly appointed and hugely proud of it and that became part of our lives really. He would be very dutiful and go to all the meetings he had to go to; eventually he was on all the committees. He was a responsible Governor. He took it very seriously and loved it. I used to go to as many functions as I could, certainly the end of year and any of the seasonal plays and stuff they put on, including going for three weeks to Australia with the school in 1988.

'A mass of us went to visit six other public schools round Australia. Richard didn't actually tell them who I was because we were farmed out to other masters in the schools that we went to. We arrived at this teacher's house because we had been billeted there and we were put in separate rooms and we sort of went "oh" and they said, "We didn't know who you were. We thought you were a teacher, Miss Cropper."

'It was *The Boyfriend*, *A Midsummer Night's Dream*, rugby and cricket, and the string orchestra. The school was mixed. We were there for three weeks and there were many performances. It was a fantastic thing and every time we saw *The Boyfriend* or *A Midsummer Night's Dream* we used to hold hands. We were so into it and so proud of them. We had a really good trip, it was brilliant. Richard was very much in love with me, and I with him.

'The ferret was more famous than anything else. The ferret was international. He used to take a video of the ferret with him so that they could play it on the local TV stations in various towns and then interview him. In Australia we used to get people coming up to him. We even got a film crew out one time, there was some Yorkshire Brass band playing at the Opera House but on the day of the filming he couldn't hear anything because of an ear infection. So I had to make all the arrangements.

'Every time we went to Gigg, which was a lot, if there was some do on or concert or something, we'd usually end up at Russell Harty's cottage which was in the village. Russell had been Richard's teacher and was Warwick and Susan Brookes's best man. If it was during the day, I very often used to take up lunch with me as in cheese and bread and pâté. Or a lady used to come in and leave stuff for Russ and Jamie, his boyfriend. So we'd go for supper and stay the night. I think Richard was a bit in awe of Russell and Russell pretended to be very cross with Richard for being made a Governor as he hadn't been made a Governor. But they were good together.

We used to have such a laugh. Russ was good fun. He was a very big gossip, anything to do with anybody he had met, he was so disdainful about everybody and extremely funny and up to the minute. Of course, Richard was always up to the minute, as I was in a way because I wanted to keep up. Warwick and Susan would be there and Hugh, the organist, and sometimes Alan Bennett. He kept himself to himself but we used to see him quite a bit. I remember cooking for them all one night at Susan's when Alan was around.

'All through the eighties was lovely – we were very happy and I absolutely loved our life together, I loved him. Things became difficult later and obviously James, his son, was the trigger for this. Richard sat down at the kitchen table with me one Friday evening in May, I think, 1988. He just said, "I have got a son." I think that's all he said. I was too shocked to begin to reply but then he said, "I have got to go to the christening tomorrow." I told him, "I have got to come too." But he was adamant that he should go alone.

'I can't remember if Richard came back that night. That's when things changed in our relationship. During the week, I got up really early, he got up late, he came in late, I went to bed early, so often we wouldn't see each other. There was a certain coolness. If Richard was in trouble with me or we had fallen out, then he would make himself scarce so that's what happened. It was quite normal not to talk about things. We didn't sit down and have big discussions. It didn't make any difference really except that if Richard was bothered about something he wouldn't tell me. However, the strain had been showing for several months.

'Then I suppose round about 1990 I started at Asda in quite a high-pressured job and life was extremely hectic for me and for him. He must have started the *Calendar* Politics show in London on Thursdays around then. I would leave home early, he would take the train to London and then I wouldn't see him again or know when I was going to see him again until he came home. So he'd go off on Thursday morning, and come back – he could come back Thursday night, Friday night, Sunday night or Monday. I had no idea. No telephone, nothing. He would sometimes ring and let me know there was a party on, but sometimes he wouldn't come home for a week and then I would sort of get to know that he had taken James to his timeshare at Denia in Spain.

'Richard didn't think he was doing anything wrong and I'm not the sort to lose my temper. I would ask him where he had been and he would either walk away or he'd say he'd seen Iain or whatever, rather than have a big row every time. This went on for about three years or so until it became obvious our relationship wasn't going to work. It took a while for us to break up after more than 12 years. I had done a lot to our house. I loved that house. I had been through the extensions, refurnished it and everything and made it a very nice home and we had had a lot of good times there. And I didn't want to leave, and I didn't want to leave him particularly. Also with such a busy job your head doesn't get time to catch up.

'However, I could not live like this. He was happy to live like that because he didn't know anything was wrong and anytime I said anything about any friction or anything like that, he would say, "Look, Jen, everybody knows that we are together, everybody knows you are the most important person in my life." So anyway it was his 50th and as part of his 50th we went to Australia. I wasn't happy going but I went. We stayed at the Ritz-Carlton in Sydney and the agent for *Countdown*, Marcel Stellmann, and his wife, Jeanie, were staying there and Michael Parkinson was staying there so there was a bit of a party going on. But Jeanie said to me: 'You're not very happy.' It wasn't the best holiday. But we had a good time mainly because one of our friends had the biggest boat in Sydney and he used to come and pick us up.

'So we came back from Australia and that's when I decided that the situation was ludicrous. I loved our life together but the house was certainly a big wrench and so once I got over that hurdle it became a bit easier. So, unbeknown to anyone else, I started looking at houses. It took me about ten days to find a new place to live. After I agreed to buy somewhere, I then told Richard that I had bought a flat in Ilkley. He said,

"That's a really good idea, that's fine" but we just carried on and I didn't move out until July because the sale took so long to complete. I can remember the week before there was a party at the Feathers and I later learnt that three of the girls in turn – Carole Tudor, Sue Clarke and Sarah Cockcroft – went and sat next to Richard at some point and said, if you don't f****** marry her or if you don't stop her from buying that flat, you're going to lose her for good. Apparently Richard just couldn't say anything. He wouldn't talk to anyone.

'Richard said he wasn't going to be there when I moved out and so I just took the things that I needed and that also wouldn't ruin the home. I'm happy to say that, after a while, we became friends and remained so up until his death.'

TWELVE

L et me jump ahead in time so that I can give you a personal account of behind-the-scenes at *Countdown*.

One Monday morning I was literally cleaning the fridge out and the phone went. It was Dick. He said: 'You'll have to come and do Dictionary Corner, the "guest" hasn't turned up.' I said: 'Don't be ridiculous.' And he said: 'No, no really I am being serious, I am sending a car for you, you've got to do it.' I said: 'Why?' People always used to say: 'Aren't you ever going on *Countdown*?' I would say, 'No, you'll never catch me there, we want to keep that separate.'

But on this occasion he said: 'No, Kathy, you will really have to come. I mean, really. There's nobody else to do it.'

We had been there before. Once all the guests for David Frost's *Through the Keyhole*, another YTV production, had been stuck on the M1 motorway and the producer literally scoured the building looking for substitutes, coming up with Richard and Jimmy Savile. When they couldn't find another, Richard suggested they pull me in, which they did.

'But my hair's a mess and I don't have any clothes,' I protested, knowing that I would have to record five *Countdown*s with five separate outfits.

'Don't worry about that, just come,' Richard pleaded.

Of course I did. I drove down the A1 to Leeds, racking my brain for five anecdotes that I could tell in the successive programmes. I don't think I've ever had such a warm welcome at YTV and was whisked into make-up for a shampoo and beauty session. Wardrobe arrived with racks of blouses quickly followed by the producers, Damian Eadie and Michael Wylie, who were solicitous of my needs and had even prepared anecdotes I might use.

In fact, I didn't need them. I simply told stories about Dick. Like the time we were in South Africa and had gone on safari. There was a bird deck outside our lodge and Richard, having got up early, came rushing back into our room insisting: 'Kathy, Kathy, there is this most incredible bird. You must come and see it.' I leapt out of bed and followed him to the deck and looked around. 'Where is it?' I asked. 'There!' He pointed upward to a tree where an upside-down, brightly coloured Woolworths bag was caught in the branches. Richard had forgotten to put his spectacles on.

Richard was always proud of *Countdown* and particularly the way in which everyone on the show respected the contestants and the audience, both in the studio and at home. He loved the fact that both producers in the last ten years of the programme were contestants years before. Michael Wylie was in the very first series of *Countdown* and he made it to the final, losing to Joyce Cansfield – the first winner. He worked in a betting shop in Edinburgh so his instant calculations rivalled Carol's. In the eighties he used to come down from Edinburgh to help the producer John Meade, and when John left he settled in Leeds and moved into the producer role himself. Damian Eadie, whom you may have seen in Dictionary Corner, won the 28th series and John interviewed him for a job as a researcher. This consisted of taking him to the bar – a place with which John was not unacquainted and asking him: 'Do you suffer from PMT?'

Damian assured him that he didn't and was hired and instructed to buy another round. So Damian not only changed his career because of *Countdown* but he also met his wife Clare who used to work on the catering for the programme. Clare and he now have three sons and he moved back to his native Blackpool and now commutes by train, a two-hour journey each way!

I must have been adequate because the producers invited me back to Dictionary Corner on five further occasions, even when there wasn't a missing guest. I think they knew I was content to be the butt of their humour – Richard re-introduced me with the words: 'Back, not by popular demand, but the demand of her bank manager, it's Kathryn Apanowicz.' We had some fairly familiar banter on screen that could have seemed strange to viewers who did not know we were partners in private.

'This is my worst nightmare,' Richard confided to the camera, while glancing from me to Carol. 'I am surrounded by both my wives.'

He could be quite tart when I was on.

Me (desperately trying to find the meaning if a word): 'I'm trying.'

Richard: 'Yes, you're very trying.'

One particularly graceless farewell was: 'Coming next week is Susie Dent and not back by popular demand is Kathryn Apanowicz. We only got her because she stays locally and is a cheap taxi.'

After finishing the five shows with two five-minute breaks, a fifteen-minute tea break and an hour for supper – during all of which we would change outfits – I felt more tired than trying – in fact, absolutely knackered. I used to be a bit unsympathetic to Richard complaining about his exhaustion after three days and fifteen shows, because I had done three- and four-hour radio and television shows and they weren't that gruelling. He used to get a bit grumpy when he came home at the end of it. I felt the same after one day, although I was a lot younger than him and I didn't have as much to think about or as much to do as he did. He had to keep the whole thing moving the whole time, so I have to say I had a great deal more understanding of his exhaustion and respect for his concentration.

Even when I was on *Countdown*, I gave him his own space on recording days as he couldn't be distracted. He spent the morning with the newspapers, a habit he never lost, and then was driven to the studios. There was a buffet lunch for the programme team, where Richard would be briefed – the producers would hand him a selected pile of letters to go through – and meet that day's guest. In his dressing room there were racks of jackets and ties for him to choose from. Initially the jackets had come from a company in Lincoln but, as the years wore on, we would buy anything with a good strong colour or bold stripe. Very often they turned up in places like Dubai or South Africa. He liked ties that were designed by Gene Meyer in New York, a taste acquired by Jon Snow on Channel 4 news.

When we ate out in restaurants if Richard was wearing a boring jacket, people would often ask him where the loud ones were and he would politely explain that they were his costume for the show – not him. The more the press commented on them and the more Terry Wogan in his Radio Two morning show sent up the 'deckchairs' Richard was wearing, the more garish Richard would become.

Once the cameras rolled, one of Richard's main concerns was that the guest in Dictionary Corner would deliver. He needed good anecdotes, wit and plenty of energy in the measure that Barry Cryer or Gyles Brandreth could be relied upon to deliver. If the guest was unprepared – and I could but won't name one extremely famous TV personality who made little or no effort – then it was like driving a car with the brake on. The other elements in the show were constants: the game would be played according to the rules, Carol would provide beauty and brilliance and banter, the contestants would provide the intensity, Susie Dent knowledge and charm and the God of Puns would incessantly smile upon Richard.

Contestants rarely got too upset about losing. There was, after all, no big money reward and being on *Countdown* was prize enough. On a couple of occasions a player scored nul points and this did seem a shame. One lady was still on zero for the conundrum at the end. The jumbled letters spelt 'REAL CHIPS' and the solution was 'SPHERICAL'. To Richard's relief she was the first to press the buzzer. 'Jennifer, at last,' he said with a smile and Jennifer replied: 'PILCHARDS.'

The thing that gave him most pleasure was when the little man beat the big man. He came home exhilarated when a professor who spoke eleven languages was beaten by a man who made Eccles cakes.

Richard had studied the original French version of the show, *Des Chiffres et Des Lettres* which attracted a large audience but was conducted in a dry, schoolmasterly way, and knew that the British preferred something more casual and much warmer. So, in a way, he Woganised it. *Countdown* remained in an era of amateurism – hence no real prizes – and fundamental good sportsmanship. What other nation could have invented Richard's favourite sport – cricket – which at Test level was played over five days and frequently ended with neither side winning. The cunning art of British *Countdown* was that it was cocooned in a time-warp and whereas, in other countries, everything became computerised down to the pads on the contestants' desk, *Countdown* à la Whiteley over its 23 years ignored the microchip revolution and still had letters on cards and felt pens all round.

The only concession to modern technology is the 'pen cam' which enables Susie or whoever is manning the dictionary to show usually a rare word on camera. It also shows the word above and the word below. Once Damian was illustrating the fact that there really was a word called 'fucoid' – it means 'relating to the seaweed fucus' – and viewers were treated to the four-letter Anglo-Saxon word that preceded it.

Incidentally, when a naughty word does come up and is in the dictionary, the contestant is rewarded with the points but they re-record the round finding a nicer word of the same length. Among the words that the teatime audience has been spared are 'arsehole', 'gobshite' and 'wankers'. I hope you are not reading this book before the nine o'clock watershed.

Richard and I went over to Paris in the spring of 2001 where he gamely agreed to appear in a *Chiffres et Lettres* special, despite only having a schoolboy command of French. When the moderator asked him if there was any difference between their version and the British one, Richard wanted to say 'We laugh' – 'Nous rions.' Unfortunately it came out as 'Nous? Rien?' – meaning no difference, so our chums across the Channel will never know.

I think what created the unique audience for *Countdown* was that it was defined by people who were able to sit down and watch telly at (originally) 4.30 p.m. or the repeat at 4.55 a.m. the next morning. Traditionally these include schoolchildren and students, waiters and taxi drivers, pensioners and the unemployed. But other, less probable, categories came to light. For instance, footballers who had finished training and, more specifically, their managers. Gordon Strachan, manager of Coventry City, told Richard that football managers call each other up if they manage to get the Conundrum. 'The loneliest thing in the world,' Gordon informed him solemnly, 'is to be on your own when you get the Conundrum with nobody to tell.'

Other fans included Lord King, the former chairman of British Airways who invited us to lunch at Wartnaby and bombarded Richard with questions about the show; Victor Lownes, the former boss of the British Playboy Club, who told Richard he was so fanatical that he had the show recorded when he was at his home in New York; and, not forgetting, as we surmised, the Queen, whose sister told Richard that her sibling tended to stay tuned to Channel 4 after the racing.

Richard's puns, by the time I came along, were not so much a programme, more a way of life. Although he became both famous and infamous for them, few people realised that they were not his idea. When he had to make the switch from being the journalistically serious presenter of *Calendar* to the light-hearted host of *Countdown*, John Meade, the producer, knew he had to bring a more jovial and amusing approach to the job. At first he hired a stand-up comedian, John Jackson, to try and train Richard in the art of quick-fire gags but this simply didn't work. It was too far from Richard's natural persona. Cambridge humour very often emanated from a play on words and he preferred this route to the other routine. So a writer, Rick Vanes, was drafted in to work with Richard on this.

Rick recalls: 'Often we would try to link the puns to the solution of the last Conundrum. So when Mark Nyman got "dagger" right, Richard introduced him in the next programme as "Mark Nyman, the World Scrabble Champion, who got 'dagger' in the Conundrum yesterday, a man as sharp as a knife, a cut above most other contestants, who is going to have a stab at coming up with more clever words." Although we collaborated, with five minutes for Richard to change clothes from one recording to the next, he rarely had time to work on this re-introduction, so it frequently went from the back of my fag packet to the Autocue where Richard would see it for the first time as he read it. And the tradition was born of him laughing at his own jokes and, on occasion, stumbling over them. Long after I and the Autocue were gone, it was still honoured.'

In the early days, when letters were few, Rick obliged in that department, too, and would try to make Dick giggle when he read out the names of correspondents such as 'Shiel Oblige from Soho'. Rick achieved a total corpse when Richard introduced a contestant, Nancy Preston, as 'having just popped up from Towcester' – pronounced 'toaster'.

Dick and I and others from the programme would sometimes eat dinner with Rick long after he had left the show. He had been a choir boy when young and, for some perverse reason, he had studied pub singers on 'Free and Easy Night' in his native Oldham. From this he had come up with a quite wonderful rendering of Frank Sinatra's 'My Way', which started out slowly but comprehensibly and then disintegrated uproariously into slurred gobbledegook as you realised the singer was pissed out of his skull. Whenever there was a microphone in a restaurant Richard would blackmail Rick into performing, to the jaw-dropping amazement of the other diners and the smothered delight of our table. Richard was once stopped in the corridor at YTV by the deputy managing director who said he had been entertaining the head of a Dutch television channel to whom he wanted to sell some YTV output in the same restaurant the previous night and was going to introduce him to 'Mr Yorkshire' but stopped in the nick of time 'when that dreadful drunk from your table started to sing.' (Rick, incidentally, doesn't drink.)

Rick left after the third series – the programme couldn't afford him – so John Meade helped Richard out with the puns. And when he left, Michael and Damian had to learn the trade. As I mentioned, the challenge was to re-introduce the guest in Dictionary Corner with some wordplay from a winning word or the conundrum that ended the previous show – a day before in transmission terms but just five minutes in recording ones, five minutes when Richard was hurriedly getting changed and selecting viewers' letters for the next show.

Dick, himself, would always note down a nifty joke based on wordplay, whatever source it came from. My favourites are:

'Two men, who are dying of thirst in the Sahara, thankfully come across a stall and beg the owner for water. "I'm sorry," the man replies, "we only sell jelly." The guys trudge on another hundred miles and are ecstatic to see another stall. Again the owner is unable to provide them with water. "We only sell hundreds and thousands," he explains. As the two men leave, one remarks to the other: "Don't you think this is a trifle strange?"'

'An anthropologist is hacking his way through the Brazilian rainforest when he comes across a lost tribe. They had cultivated a special plant that provided a cure for constipation. The anthropologist was amazed but the tribe's leader assured him: "With fronds like these who needs enemas."'

And one for luck:

'Two Eskimos were on a wooden boat and it was so cold that one of them lit a fire. Unfortunately the boat caught fire and sank which just goes to show that you can't have your kayak and eat it.'

Then of course there were the Whiteley bloopers which were normally left in as part of the entertainment unless they were misleading or libellous. In the early days Richard would present YTV's news magazine, *Calendar*, every night as well as taping fifteen *Countdowns* and towards the end of the recordings, understandably, he would suffer from a bit of brain fade and, as I mentioned earlier, once or twice, welcomed *Countdown* viewers to *Calendar*.

A professional musician became a professional 'museum' and a laboratory assistant became a 'lavatory' assistant.

But he got to be quick in correcting himself.

'I said "letters" but you should have known it was "numbers".'

'The chimp has got it – sorry, the champ has got it.'

'With eyes tut shi – sorry, shut tight.'

Sometimes his utterances were not so much a mistake but pure Whiteleyisms:

'We have a great game in store today because both contestants are called Brian – except for Andy.'

On one occasion, Damian remembers, he had written an introduction to a female contestant and mistyped her age on the introduction card. So Richard read out that she was 63 whereas she was, in fact, 36. Amazingly neither he nor any of the 150 people in the audience noticed this – a fact that did not fill her with the greatest of pleasure. There was a certain amount of embarrassed laughter when a retake was required.

The audience, it may be said, were not always in the first flush of youth – although sometimes a student union would blow into town. They came in coaches from as far away as Devon and watched either two or three shows. They were devoted viewers and were the bedrock of Richard and Carol's fan club. When I was the guest in Dictionary Corner I would sometimes try to wind up Susie Dent by writing silly little messages on my pad, just as you would do at school.

Richard, meanwhile, was publicly winding up the woman he always privately called Vorders.

'Okay, Carol, stand by your station and get ready to give Dom whatever he wants.'

Although pre-recorded, the programme always gave the viewers the impression that it was happening on the day it was transmitted, thus Richard would wear a white rose on Yorkshire Day or a poppy for Remembrance Day and one memorable Valentine's Day tricked Carol into believing she was going to get a bunch or roses and a kiss when, in fact, both went to the guest, Esther Rantzen.

Richard: The first of May, the first of May. Outdoor kissing begins today.
Carol: Did you make that up?
Richard (caught): Yes.

The wittier the guest, the more he enjoyed the banter.

Contestant: I hope 'ablution' can be singular.
Stephen Fry: Yes. One usually does one's ablutions, but one can certainly ablute in the singular.
Richard: Ablute in the singular, actually Stephen that's what I usually do.

Dick was not above being a little rebellious with the control gallery, especially if he felt they had edited one of his better puns out of a recent show to get it down to time. If, at the end of the recording, the instruction came in his ear from Cindy Ritson, the long-serving production assistant: 'Richard, can you spin it out, we have 50 seconds to fill' – the 45-minute slot required a 37-minute 10-second programme – he would, on very rare occasion say: 'Well, that's it from another *Countdown* etc.' and wrap things up in 10 seconds. Conversely, also on very rare occasions, when they needed him to end fast, he would launch into favourite soliloquies about the iniquitous price of real sponges, his love of lamb chops cooked slowly on an Aga or read from the *Wetwang Tatler* stories such as 'Sheepdog hurts paw.'

It was all good-natured horseplay. Timing was solved in the edit and, in the immortal words of Denis Norden – the catalyst of many ferret pounds into the Whiteley bank account – it was all right on the night.

One pleasing byproduct of *Countdown* was that some regular guests became friends and guests at The Parsonage, as well. People whom Richard would never otherwise have met from very different walks of life. Rick Wakeman, the rock musician, was a great fan of the show and eagerly became a participant. Sir Tim Rice was always a welcoming figure when we came to London and drove up and back in a day – 500 miles – to read a poem at Richard's funeral. Jo Brand, the stand-up comedienne, had watched the programme from the very start. 'Earlier on, my ambition was to marry Richard Whiteley,' she claims, 'but when I realised how many gorgeous women were fighting over him, I sadly had to drop any thoughts of a happy union and content myself with seeing him on the television five days a week.'

But, for 23 years, the *Countdown* team provided Richard with his office family. They were a small, tight-knit group assembled by the late, great John Meade. Michael and Damian, the producers; Cindy, the PA; and Diane Barr, the programme associate and the person who was closest to Richard.

'He could be an awkward bugger,' she recalls. 'If he was in a crabby mood I would ask him straight: "What's wrong with you?" Half the time he would smile and brighten up a bit. He would rarely tell me. He didn't bring his personal problems to the office. The only time we had to cancel a programme was when his mother died the night before. Even if he was really ill he would always do the programme. He later developed diabetes and had been an asthmatic since he was a child and, on more than one occasion, I had to call a doctor to give him something in his dressing room.

'But most days he was wonderful. He was a very tactile man. He would come up from behind and rub your shoulders and touch your hair.

'Sometimes, out of the blue, he would rub his hands together and say: "Let's all go to the Flying Pizza and have a spot of lunch." He would treat us and we knew there would be very little work done that afternoon.'

At Christmas I would help Dick wrap presents for everyone on *Countdown*, literally everyone: director, vision mixer, floor manager, cameramen, make-up, audience co-ordinators – the lot. The dining table at The Parsonage looked like Santa's grotto.

YTV would treat the main team to a Christmas lunch and Richard would give out the gifts. He would also go round the table and make a short speech about each of them. One year a secretary came back to the programme after having been away for a while. Diane whispered to Dick that she had, in fact, had breast enhancement surgery. People held their breath as he came to her. 'Welcome back, Sue,' he said, 'You are twice the woman you were.'

Although *Countdown* earned many millions pounds a year for YTV, a new management, in their wisdom, cancelled the *Countdown* Christmas lunch one year, saying the company could no longer afford such luxuries.

Richard's reaction was immediate and decisive. He paid for it himself.

THIRTEEN

Richard's creative talents were annually on display to a much smaller audience. Every Christmas he would write a pantomime for his extended family – Helen and James and their two children, Alex and George, and James's brother Peter and Christine and their two children, Lizzie and Henry. Other people would be drafted in as needed: one year Jeni's distinguished RAF Group Captain father was requisitioned to play an Ugly Sister.

It had been Christine's idea, and she made the costumes while Dick wrote the script and later she took the children through rehearsals. The families would join up for a traditional Christmas lunch after which the performance took place, with the parents well-wined and ready to be entertained. In early years the little ones didn't always understand the innuendoes that Uncle Richard was putting in their mouths but all the family fully expected – and hoped – to be insulted.

Christine has faithfully kept the original script of one such work that he wrote in the Seventies. It was called: *LITTLE*

RED RIDING HOOD AND THE BEANSTALK MEET SLEEPING BEAUTY. First off to be insulted, none too subtly, was Richard's sister, always known to him as Nellie.

ENTER JACK: Hello, Red Riding Hood. I'm off to the market to sell an old cow. She's called Nellie.

Then there was a traditional reference to how rich Peter and James's mother was and how the grandchildren always hoped to receive a little cash present when they visited her.

RED RIDING HOOD: Hello, Granny. Why are you in bed? My, what big eyes you've got! What big ears you've got!! And what a big purse you've got!!!

I think Henry, who played Jack, and Alex, as Red Riding Hood, would only have been about five and six when they had to deliver Uncle Richard's next naughty exchange.

JACK: She's going to gobble us up. Quick – here are my magic seeds.
(Sprinkles seeds and a giant beanstalk appears.)
RED RIDING HOOD: What's that huge erection? It's just like daddy's peonies.

No friend was allowed to escape Richard's sharp pen.

OLD WOMAN: What are you doing?
RED RIDING HOOD: We're fleeing from the Big Bad Wolf. He's ugly, rude and horrible.
OLD WOMAN: I didn't know Frank Marshall was around.
RED RIDING HOOD: Yes, he's in business with my brother, Robin Hood.
OLD WOMAN: He *likes* Robin?
RED RIDING HOOD: Yes – Robin the poor to give to the rich.

OLD WOMAN: You must kiss the sleeping prince. It's the only way to wake him up. Then you'll be rich. He'll tell you where there is a huge stack of money. He knows the number of John Stewart's bank account in Switzerland.

John was the eldest and, at the time, richest of the three Stewart brothers. I have appeared in a few professional pantomimes and I always felt that if Richard ever gave up the afternoon job, he could have made a living writing such fun.

Those Christmas pantomimes and parties paint the picture of an affluent family gathering, carefree and confident enough to poke fun at one another and live the good life. But in a horrible, Chekhovian way it was not to last.

The fun was not at an end yet, however. In January 1997 I got a phone call asking me if I was alone. I was. They wanted to do a *This Is Your Life* on Richard. Would I help them?

I worked closely with the producer figuring out who would be good from family, friends and work colleagues to appear on the show. When I told those involved, it surprised me how much people enjoyed a conspiracy, even when it involved telling some minor white lies to Richard.

The trap was to be a photo-shoot on the set of *Emmerdale*, the long-running Yorkshire soap opera. The idea was a generic advertisement for YTV's two most successful shows. As Richard nonchalantly posed with Malandra and the rest of the *Emmerdale* girls in Kitty's Tea Rooms, Michael Aspel hove into view with his Big Red Book and remarked: 'Flash bang, wallop, what a photograph! Can I come and be seen sharing a joke because if you do say "yes" I will then be able to say: "Tonight, Richard Whiteley, this is your life." '

Richard was already committed to attending a ceremony in memory of Bob Cryer the Labour MP who had been killed in a car crash, so the studio recording did not take place until 10.30 at night. Still, that gave the cast plenty of time to rehearse, twice with a stand-in and once with the great Aspel himself.

It was decided that Richard's mother, Margaret, should not be put through the ordeal of stepping through the portal and delivering her piece standing up. Instead, from her seat, she would reveal that her son was passionate about television as a child, from the time in 1952 when they got a Ferguson TV, and he always wanted to be a cameraman.

Terry Wogan, on tape, got the proceedings rolling. 'Richard Whiteley. The oldest man on Channel 4. The doyen of quiz shows. Dear old boy who in all those years is still the same – same jokes, same flushed appearance, same Carol. "Ferret, please, Carol" – goes out the cry. And then you meet somebody who's been watching *Countdown* and they say, "Did you watch *Countdown* this week?" and you say, "Yes I did." "And how was Richard Whiteley – no improvement?" '

Michael asked Richard why he didn't follow his father into textiles and he replied: 'Well, like a lot of kids of my age – we got a TV in 1952, a purple screen, a Ferguson, a 12-inch – just before the Coronation and I was nine and I was fascinated by television and I always wanted to work in television – I wanted to be a cameraman and had no interest in textiles really and just was keen on telly.'

Aspel then moved over to his mother. 'And Margaret, young Richard was bowled over by the telly.'

'Yes he was,' she agreed and than announced inimitably: 'And may I just say I only had three lines to say and he's said them.'

The studio collapsed in laughter.

Michael persisted: 'But you will tell us about what he did as a small boy – how did his love of cameras manifest itself?'

Margaret: 'Oh, well, he used to make cameras from cardboard boxes, and earphones – so he was destined for TV.'

In fact Whiteley, mère et fillé, pretty well stole the evening, with Helen telling the dead hamster story.

'When he went back to Giggleswick, he had to leave a rather scrawny looking hamster behind called Kimmy, and he made me look after it. For weeks and weeks I fed and watered this funny-looking animal. Till one day I went to his hutch and, low and behold, there was poor Kimmy curled up in a ball, stone cold and definitely stiff. So mother wrote to Richard and said unfortunately we have some sad news,

Kimmy is no longer with us but we've found a nice spot for him in the garden so all is well. Anyway the next day Richard got special permission by his house master to phone home. This frantic voice at the other end of the phone said – "Kimmy is not dead, dig him up, he's hibernating." So we duly dug the poor hamster up who meanwhile had been underground for three days, wrapped him in swaddling clothes and put him on top of the Aga. He took two days to come round and he lived for another two years.'

The evening ended with the Yorkshire legend, the late Fred Trueman, telling an impenetrable story and the Giggleswick School jazz singers serenading us with 'Who Could Ask For Anything More?'

At the after-show party Bruce Gyngell, the new Managing Director, transformed the wine into good champagne with a wave of the YTV company cheque book and Richard told the assembled throng as he toasted them that this was the best party that Yorkshire Television had thrown in 30 years. 'It's a funny feeling,' he said, 'you look around at all the people, laughing and drinking, and you realise that they are only there because of you, and the next time a similar crowd gather on your behalf and say nice things about you, it will probably be your funeral.'

Tragically this would turn out to be true. But, before that, there was to be other devastating news.

In 1980 a malignant melanoma was diagnosed on Helen's right arm. It was removed and she had to have a skin graft from her left arm. Some years later she had a hysterectomy and surgery for cancer of the colon. Then, in the summer of 1997, she began to lose weight rapidly. Her daughter Georgie had completed her second year at Cambridge where she was reading geography and was about to embark on a research trip to India.

'Mummy didn't want me to go. I said to her: "If you go to the doctors, I won't go to India." But she wouldn't go, so I set off for India. Weeks later I was in Simla in the foothills of the Himalayas and I rang home. They told me Mum had cancer of the liver. I was in a phone booth and I was in floods of tears and there were all these Indians surrounding it and staring at me. Then I got a flight back immediately.'

Helen embarked on a course of chemotherapy. Christine, her sister-in-law, came over to her house most days to help. Richard would visit every weekend and when he could during the week. Obviously there was nothing he could do medically but he did his best to keep up his sister's spirits and also to be supportive to James and the two girls. It was only when Helen was taken into hospital that he stopped visiting for a while. Richard couldn't bear hospitals – although when Peter, Christine's consultant husband, asked him to come with him on his Christmas Day rounds of Bradford Royal Infirmary – where Richard ended up himself – he put this fear to one side and talked jovially to the patients and staff who were surprised to meet a television personality.

Helen was let out of hospital to go home to Shaftesbury House. With the effects of the chemotherapy having worn off, there were days she felt quite well, as Georgie recalled.

'I remember her very last Sunday lunch. Richard had invited us to Spring Bank Cottage and as the four of us drove over from Bradford we listened to *My Fair Lady*, which was her favourite musical, in the car and at Uncle Richard's we sang songs like 'The Sun has Got His Hat On'. It was a lovely, lovely day. It just seemed like everything was normal. Mummy was on such good form that it just seemed impossible that she was going to die.'

But by the end of that week she had begun to weaken badly. Christine, who had been administering morphine and monitoring her condition, told Georgie to ring Richard and tell him to come to Shaftesbury House. When he got there she warned him this might be the last time he saw his sister so he went to spend some time with her alone in her bedroom.

'I had to disturb him eventually,' said Christine, 'so that Alex and Georgie could go in and say goodbye. I opened the door gently. Helen was conscious and Richard was sitting on a chair by the bed reading her *Milly Molly Mandy* just as he used to do when they were children.'

Milly Molly Mandy was the story of a young girl who lived

in a thatched cottage in a sleepy English village, together with her mother, father, grandpa, grandma, uncle, and an aunty. The simple tales, such as her toffee-making and dressing-up, are a reminder of the innocence of bygone childhood.

They then had prayers around the bed with Helen's husband, mother, brother and two children all holding hands.

'I remember after that Uncle Richard just going and sitting on the stairs,' Georgie said. 'He didn't really know where to go. Mummy became a little restless and Alex and I left the room. It was just before she died. We went and sat on the stairs with Richard and I remember him putting his arms around us and feeling that warmth from him. He just totally forgot about himself and looked after the two of us. I remember that really vividly and that was the start of a very close bond. We had been really close up until then but that was the start of a new relationship between Richard and Alex and myself.'

It was Richard who telephoned Bradford Cathedral and told them that his sister, the wife of the son of Henry Stewart, Freeman of the City, had died and the family would like to hold her funeral there.

Seven hundred people turned up the following Friday. Helen had many friends. Richard helped usher them to their seats and then gave the most touching address about his sister, Nellie. He described how she had lit up so many people's lives, even when she was ill. Looking at the vast assembly who had turned out to say goodbye to her he recalled the time he was about to go to the funeral of some MP and Helen, in her usual straight talking way, told him: 'I don't know why you're going to *his* funeral, he wouldn't go to yours.'

In a horrible coincidence, Richard's first Yorkshire girl-friend, Jennie Greenwood, died on 21 February 1998 of ovarian cancer, two weeks before Helen.

That Christmas James and the girls and Richard's mother came to stay at The Parsonage. No pantomimes any more but lots of wine, singing and laughter. Georgie said that she had the best of times.

Richard now felt he had an added responsibility to his nieces. 'In a way he saw himself as being mummy's ambassador,' Georgie explained. 'He would ring me regularly at Cambridge to see how I was. Me more than Alex, probably, because she was moving into a professional life and had a boyfriend whereas I was a bit younger and didn't. He even came to support me in the *Varsity* lacrosse match.'

Dick and I joined James and Alex at Georgie's graduation in 1999. She was at St Catharine's College and for some reason the BBC were filming a documentary about it. As it happened, the daughter of Michael Howard, the politician, was graduating on the same day as Georgie. The BBC swooped on him and Dick asking for interviews but Richard told them, 'I'm not having you interview me, this is nothing to do with me. If you want to interview me, you interview me with my niece.' Which they did.

With Helen gone, Richard looked after his mother as, indeed, she had looked after him until quite late in life. When he was living alone in Spring Bank Cottage in Burley Woodhead, she would come and collect his laundry and do it for him. He would pay her for this. On one occasion he asked if she could wait for next time as he had literally no money on him. 'That's all right,' said Margaret, 'I take Visa or American Express.'

He paid for her to live in sheltered housing and visited her each Friday and did her paperwork until she died in September 2001.

Alex followed in her father's footsteps as a promising barrister. When she got married in April 2002 to Alistair Brook, she chose to do so at St Mary's Church in Masham where she had worshipped as a child when her family were staying with Uncle Richard. Afterwards they came to us at The Parsonage and James held a splendid reception and dinner dance for them in a marquee in the garden.

Alex was by now 27 and her expectation of life was increased into her mid-thirties according to the dread actuarial statistics for people with cystic fibrosis. But her mother's death had hit her hard and she began to fade. She died in June 2003 at Seacroft Hospital surrounded by her husband Alistair, her family and friends and, like Helen, her funeral was held in Bradford Cathedral.

James had now lost a wife and a daughter within five years. At one stage he wanted to give up law and just get away. But he was prevailed upon to become a County Court Judge and Richard was his guest at his 'screening in' at the House of Lords. James became a frequent visitor, usually spending each weekend with us.

'Richard and I talked a lot about Helen,' he said. 'He never talked about himself. He always asked me lots of questions. We would discuss politics a lot, although he never revealed whom he voted for. He kept the same impartiality as he had when he was a political interviewer but I think he was conservative with a small "c".'

After Richard died, Judge James got remarried to Deborah who, herself, had lost a son. And four years to the day after Alex was married, Georgie was married to Tim Brewis, a former army officer who now taught with her at Cheltenham Ladies College. Like Alex, she chose St Mary's, Masham, and like Alex her reception was held here at The Parsonage.

During the week leading up to the ceremony Georgie and her two bridesmaids, Lotte and Hermione, stayed in our converted stables, Ferret Hall, and there were nights of great laughter as they demolished several bottles of champagne that were stored there.

Richard would have loved to join in.

FOURTEEN

To Richard's chagrin he was never asked to be a guest on *Desert Island Discs*. But he would have hated to be cast away on a desert island. He loved travel but to him meeting new people was just as important as seeing new sights.

Iain Johnstone has a theory that Richard actually attracts oddball characters on these trips. Because Richard was somewhat miffed at not being asked to be Best Man at Iain's second wedding, his new wife Mo suggested that he might like to go on honeymoon with them to Ibiza. In those days in the 70s, it was necessary to change planes at Valencia Airport in southern Spain and take another one for the Balearics. As they were waiting there an elderly Yorkshireman with his luggage came up to Richard, recognising him from *Calendar*. 'I bet you don't know what's in this suitcase,' he said. Richard supposed it contained his holiday clothes and possibly books. 'No,' replied the old chap, opening it with a flourish, 'pork pies – I don't trust that Spanish cooking.' And it was indeed full to overflowing with these delicacies.

Once installed in Santa Eulalia where they had rented an apartment, Richard quickly smelt out Sandy's Bar. This proved to be a place where British actors who were 'between jobs' would come for a mid-morning drink. But there was another purpose: Sandy had one of the few phones on the island and that was where actors could be contacted with job offers. Dick would do a great impression of a confirmed bachelor thesp entering the bar with a cry of: 'Sandy, has my agent called?' and the queen behind the bar would reply: 'Not today, darling,' whereupon the actor would turn on him angrily: 'Well, *why* not?'

On the last holiday the two men spent together in January of the year Richard died, Iain came to stay with us at Villa Liliana in Portugal. Dick drove him back to the airport and as Iain was checking in, asked a woman in the queue behind him if she had enjoyed her holiday. 'It wasn't a holiday,' said the woman, 'I lived here but now I'm going back to live in England.' 'That's a shame,' Richard replied, 'I've just bought a place here and I think it's wonderful. What was wrong?' The woman shook her head. 'You just can't get Campbell's Tomato Soup.'

Another culinary problem. In fact you can get Campbell's Tomato Soup in the Apollonia Hypermarket in Almancil but Richard felt that it was a bit late to pass on this information.

Despite their months of silence as they sat beside each other at YTV – or maybe in a strange way because of them – Richard and Bob Warman became steadfast friends once Bob had returned to the safe harbour of ATV. They loved to go on holiday together and Bob loved to reminisce about them.

'It was the year of the Brighton bombings – 1984 – and we went off to Australia. We had a terrific holiday together starting off in Sydney and then we went up the Barrier Reef, a bit of Outback and finally back to Sydney. There, one night in a bar, we bumped into a PR man from Qantas and the subject got round to what we were doing in Australia. Richard always at that time carried the famous tape of his ferret attack and he told the chap he was about to go on Channel 9 television the following morning armed to show the bloop of the ferret. This PR man from Qantas said: "Ah well, Rich, tell

Above
Christmas with mother.

Above
Goddaughter Holly's 21st.

Below
Paul Ashford (Pub-Pot), Ricco and Bobbo.

Above
'Come fly with me!' Yes, we actually went paragliding.

Below
'It looked easy in Jamie Oliver's book'

bove
New Year with Christine Stewart.

Above
Judge James with his daughters
Alex, in white, and Georgie.

Below
The Mayor of Wetwang.

Above
Beloved niece, Georgina.

Above
With John Willis – separated at birth.

Below
Not so much Him-off, more nod-off.

On board the QE2: Chris Tarrant, Richard, Lorraine Kelly, Nicholas Parsons and Jeremy Beadle

With Kenneth and brother-in-law, James Stewart

Above
He always loved 'The Desert Song.'

Above
A kiss from Lord Kirkham.

Below
Dick was never good with spaghetti; a bib was essential.

bove
n the piste at The Parsonage.

Above
His TV wife.

elow
*V*ith Sir Paul Fox and Lady Betty.

Left
His proudest moment.

Below
At York Minster.

you what, get the name Qantas in and we'll give you both business class on the way back."

'Now we had flown down to Sydney in the boot and it's a long way – and business class all the way back to the UK was a prize indeed. So I said to him later, "Ricco, whatever you do you have got to get that name Qantas in somehow." And he said, "Leave it to me, leave it to me, I'll find a way of doing it."

'The following morning I was in the hotel bedroom and I switched on the television to watch Richard on the breakfast show. He was interviewed about the ferret, they showed the bit about the ferret biting his finger and so on. It was a very fast-moving show and the presenter said, "Rich, that's great, it's great to have you along here and thanks for joining us." And I thought, Christ, he hasn't mentioned Qantas yet. I could see a flash of panic come across Richard's face, and he said, "Well, don't you want to know why I am here?" "You're on holiday aren't you, Rich?" He replied, "There's more to it than that. I was there at the time of the Brighton bombing."

'And I was wondering how on earth was he going to get Qantas into this? But he went on. "I was actually there, in the hotel, when the explosion happened. I was so relieved to get out of it, I thought this is the first day of the rest of my life, and I walked into the nearest Qantas office and booked a flight to Australia."

'And I thought, you've cracked it baby, and we did and we got business class.

Our favourite European destination was the Algarve. So when the BBC holiday programme invited Richard to do an item for them, he asked for a house in the hills above Sao Bras, well away from the coast where young Brits dance the night away at "Val de Yobbo". The camera crew followed him to the barbers, having lunch in his favourite chicken restaurant and pottering about the market. He had written an outline script for the programme, which included the words: "At the end of the day I like to have a few friends over for drinks on the sun deck." This presented a problem: at the time of filming hardly anyone we knew was in Portugal, except for Iain and his family. So Dick made an emergency call to him and Iain duly rounded up all the people who were sunbathing round the Roman colonnaded pool at Dunas Douradas. They drove up the winding hill like a tank corps to the rescue. The BBC camera rolled but fortunately on a long lens from a distance, or else they would have heard the star of the show saying to his "friends", "And who exactly are you?" The programme was repeated over the years and many people reported back to Iain telling him that friends or relatives had said to them, "I didn't know you were a friend of Richard Whiteley's."

Before that he used to go to Portugal with Bob. 'Portugal was when we were at our most relaxed and when I say relaxed, I suppose that was when we were doing most of our drinking which would start off at about 11 o'clock in the morning with a couple of quick chasers. One day we were going to have a barbecue and off we went to the market in Sao Bras where Richard said, "I am going to introduce you to the butcher who produces the finest legs of lamb that you will have ever tasted." Of course we stopped by the bar and had a couple of swift ones first. The butcher's was looking very crowded at the time so we went and had a couple more and thought we would wait until the queue had gone down a bit.

'So, reasonably sozzled, we went into the butchers. She was a very attractive female butcher, she didn't look like a butcher, she looked like a diva. Anyway Richard wasn't really looking and he pointed at various things on the counter and we bought these supposedly two very fine legs of lamb. That evening we get the barbecue going, the coals are firing away and on go the legs of lamb when one of our friends, a Yorkshireman, Paul Ashford, said, "What are these bloody things you've got, Richard?" Richard said, "Legs of lamb." And Paul said. "Ah, since when did bloody lambs have feathers sticking out of them?" We had bought two whacking great turkey legs. Richard just curled up in a ball and couldn't stop laughing.'

The next year Bob and Paul went a couple of days ahead of Richard. 'When he arrived,' Paul remembered, 'it just wasn't him. He was quiet, no laughter, no jokes. His mind seemed to be somewhere else. I asked him what was wrong and he said that I would find out sooner or later but he had fathered a child after a one-night stand with some woman at the Scarborough cricket festival. He told Bob as well, but none of the girls. He was very cut-up but he didn't want to talk about it further and we respected that.'

Richard looked after his son, James, very generously for the rest of his life. Being an honourable man, over the years he built up a loving relationship with James. He came to stay with us during his holidays.

A prerequisite for Richard in any Portuguese villa was a satellite television. He couldn't bear to be separated from his first love – or the latest news. One year Georgie came down to stay with us and still dines out on this tale.

'They hired a villa, it was before they owned their own, and I remember I was there for a week and it was during the World Cup rugby in Australia. Uncle Richard said to me one night, "Oh we've got some guests coming round tomorrow to watch the rugby on our Sky TV." I said, "Oh right, who is it?" And he goes mysteriously, "It's someone on telly.' I, somewhat cheekily, asked, "Is it someone like William G. Stewart or some armchair celebrity like you?" And he said, "Oh, no. You will be surprised."

'The next morning the bell rang and he says, "Go on then, you go and get it." So I went and opened the door and there was Johnny Vaughn standing there who at the time was incredibly famous – he was a really big cheese in those days. I couldn't believe it. He goes "Hello" and I went, "Hi, I'm Georgie," and he goes, "I'm Johnny." Then he came in with these two other big burly chaps and they sat down. Uncle Richard suddenly started to become really laddie and he was like, "Come on lads, yeah, rugby is about to start." Kathy and I just went, "This isn't quite like the Richard we know" and they all slumped on the sofas and turned on the telly and Richard's going, "Got any lagers, Georgie?" I have never known Richard drink a lager in his life and I went to look in the fridge and I said, "We don't have lager, Uncle Richard." He goes, "Do you mind popping down to the supermarket?" So Kathy and I sniggered and went off to the supermarket, came back with a crate of lager and there they were all sitting there drinking it on the sofa. I remember that very well. He was such a prat that day but so endearingly lovely. That was so like him, he just wanted to be friendly to everybody and make himself like the other person so they would feel comfortable.'

Many years later when we were renting a car at Faro Airport in Portugal, the girl said, 'I've just been watching you.'

'Really,' Richard began, 'which . . .'

But she interrupted him with a finger which she pointed at me. 'Not you, you. I've been watching old episodes of *Angels* on UK Gold.' Dick was a little taken aback, then rather proud.

I can tell when these are repeated; I usually get a cheque for 79p each time.

Always welcome, more than welcome, was an invitation from Lord and Lady Kirkham to join them on their yacht – it sleeps ten with a crew of 13 to look after them. Last time we were anchored off the island of Capri. A tender took us to shore and then we were curiously guarded by the crew on the way to the restaurant. It seemed somewhat strange, but in fact Graham had a surprise in store. We arrived at a hotel for pre-dinner cocktails and heard wonderful singing coming from the street. I thought it was buskers but in fact Graham had especially flown in the speciality act, Three Waiters, from London. This treat was made up of three opera singers and was why the crew had guarded us, they didn't want to spoil the surprise. We then went along to another restaurant where our table was next to some crusty Americans who asked us to be a little quieter. I asked them to join us as it was my husband's birthday (of course it wasn't, it was just a ruse to get them to lay off). The waiters in the restaurant heard this and immediately produced a birthday cake complete with fireworks. We thought this was amazing but when Richard tried to cut into the cake we discovered that it was made of cardboard which raised a hell of a lot of laughs.

Richard and Graham Kirkham loved nothing more than a sing-song and on the way out of the restaurant who should be sitting in the corner but Mariah Carey and Queen Latifah who happily joined in with the party. The crusty Americans were silenced.

We moved on to a nightclub, where everybody was already singing. The tenors said they wanted to sing 'Nessum Dorma' and the Italians were a bit snooty about this. But when they heard it, the roof was raised. Whether they enjoyed my rendition of 'Fly Me to the Moon' or Graham's 'Wonderful World' I cannot remember. What I do remember was that it was just about the best night out I ever had. I didn't want the party to end.

In New York, Barbara Taylor Bradford and her husband Bob were always good to us. Barbara Taylor, as she was, came from Leeds and was a reporter on the *Yorkshire Evening Post*. When she had her breakthrough as a novelist with *A Woman of Substance* in 1976, she became a regular on *Calendar* and a friend of Richard's. To date, she has sold more than 75 million books. She didn't take the surname Bradford out of any allegiance to Yorkshire, incidentally; it was simply the surname of her American husband. Bob could always get us into things when we were in Manhattan. Richard loved Broadway and went wide-eyed at *The Music Man* and *Crazy For You*. The Bradfords would take us for dinner. Once at Le Cirque I remember a waiter presenting Bob with a bill – or the check. 'I don't do checks,' said Bob. He had accounts nearly everywhere.

The only time we went to Los Angeles was on the way home from Australia and the weather was foul. So we went to the movies. It was a full house and the film was Nick Hornby's *About a Boy*. The rich and idle leading man, played by Hugh Grant, divides his life into half-hours, one of which was devoted to watching *Countdown*. I wanted to say to the people on our row, 'This is him' but Richard restrained me.

Richard had begun a routine of taking all of February off so we could go to South Africa. On our trip to a game reserve we took the train from Johannesburg to Port Elizabeth. Dinner was served on board and there were only two other people in our compartment. 'If you meet people, there will be something in common,' Richard whispered to me like some sort of Celestine prophet. Sure enough they were English and the man worked for Granada Television.

At the game reserve who should turn up but David Gower and his family. He was over there commentating on the Test match. Dick decided to play a prank on him. David was staying at the presidential suite and so Dick got one of the rangers to tell David that whoever stayed there was obliged to give a cocktail party. Which David duly did and I must say when he learnt he'd been set up, he took it extremely well.

And then there was Australia, Richard's first love since he had been there as a student. Sydney and Queensland had become almost familiar to us, so we penetrated the Outback and Richard was anxious to take me to Broome which he had visited for the BBC. First, though, we went to see the Bungle Bungles in Purnululu National Park in Western Australia. This range was used by Aboriginals during the wet season, when plant and animal life was abundant, but few Europeans knew of its existence until the mid-1980s.

The Bungle Bungles, Richard remarked, so good that, like New York, they named it twice. They are in fact huge mounds of rock, bubbling out of the ground like giant beehives.

These hundreds of brownish and yellowish rounded rocks are geological marvels. We flew over them on our way to Bellburn camp, our base for a first-hand examination of this prehistoric land called the Kimberly. To really appreciate the lonely terrain, you have to walk it. They made it as comfortable as they could. Robert, our ranger, met our party of four at the dirt airstrip. He proved to be a man who knew no fear – in the rainy season he escorted trippers up and down Sydney Harbour Bridge.

He warned us of the 36 hours ahead. "You'll be hot, very hot, thirsty, very thirsty, and by the end of the day, you'll be tired, very very tired."

After a hearty breakfast cooked in a tent by a couple of cheerful girls who pretended not to know what we were in for, we boarded a bus and set out into the unknown.

Robert drove us cheerfully along the red dirt roads, the great red sandstone rocks always on the horizon. It was a day of walking along dried-up river beds, entering huge gorges, lunching in cathedral-like grottoes, walking to spectacular viewpoints, stopping at intervals for huge gulps of water. For Yorkshire's least athletic man, this could have been something of a challenge, but, with a good pair of boots to master the rocky terrain, the trek was safe, even though, like the mad dogs we Englishmen are, we were out in 45 degrees of midday sun.

We enjoyed our sundowners sitting in the shade of the bus, watching the sun set over the mountain ranges. Back at the camp in the gathering gloom, we peeled off and showered in the open air. Teeth were cleaned in an outside sink and the dunny was a hole in the ground.

In the main tent, the girls were cooking a comforting meal, and we were back in our tents, listening to the sounds of the Outback by eight o'clock. By 8.30 the generators were switched off, and we slept soundly, at peace with the world.

Next day it was farewell to Bellburn Camp, but not without an optional extra, a helicopter trip over the Bungle Bungles.

To sit in a little aircraft with no doors, strapped in only by a lap belt as you swoop into mountain gorges and skim along the tops of deep chasms, demands some trust in the pilot. "Aw, yer won't fall out, centrifugal force will see to that," he cheerfully called through the headphones. It was only on landing that we discovered that gorge-swooping was not his real job; in the wet season he was a butcher in Sydney.

Richard had booked us in at the Seashells resort in Broome, a collection of apartments grouped around a lovely pool and stunning gardens.

Broome, 800 miles from Darwin, is a town with an intriguing history. It was the centre of the world pearling industry for 50 years. At the turn of the 19th century it was a tough town of divers and ruthless bosses. The divers, mainly Japanese, donned huge and hefty diving suits and worked in ever-worsening conditions, as their greedy bosses forced them to dive deeper and deeper in search of the oysters.

The graveyard is a moving witness to the hundreds of them who never surfaced alive.

Broome's star attraction is its beach. Cable Beach is so called because Australia's telegraphic link with the outside world was established there – a cable link with Indonesia. It's huge expanse of shiny, white, hot sand that just goes on and on – surely one of the world's best-kept secrets.

But the star attraction is the 'Stairway to Heaven'.

We stood on the shore watching the moon rise out of the sea. It gave off a shaft of light that grew stronger and brighter. It was unlike any other reflection you have ever seen, not wavy or fidgety but dead straight, a perfect geometrical ladder of light leading straight from the full face of the moon, right across the calm sea, almost to within touching distance.

This illusion happens only a few times a year, when the moonrise and the tides are in a distinct pattern. We had arrived in Broome after a 10,000-mile journey, just in time.

We watched in a hushed crowd, gathered to witness this unique sight. In the background, a didgeridoo droned hauntingly. We held hands, slightly tearfully. It was a romantic moment on the other side of the world.

And then, the hush was broken by a familiar accent.

'Well, Richard Whiteley! You've just saved me two dollars. I was going to send you a postcard. Bryan and I have just been working out what we miss about Yorkshire: number one was Marks & Spencer sausage rolls, and number two was *Countdown*. I was just going to write to tell you, and now you're here. I can't believe it.'

How I will miss just the best holiday companion.

FIFTEEN

S ince *Countdown* recordings could be compressed into 50 days a year, Richard was always game for a challenge on some other television shows. One of the most attractive of these was to be sent to Australia to become a 'Flying Postie' in a new reality series called *Danger – Celebrity at Work* hosted by Fern Britton for the BBC.

'In Queensland's vast outback, the Flying Postman provides not only the mail, but a vital lifeline,' Fern told the viewers. 'So when we asked Richard Whiteley to be our Flying Postie, he took a somewhat romantic view of the job ahead.'

'If I had to give up my teatime desk job, this is perhaps the only job in the world that would tear me away,' said Richard, his tongue nearly penetrating his cheek. He couldn't resist adding a trademark pun: 'Besides, I do know a thing or two about letters!'

But, as has been observed, he knew very little about maths and when he found his first task was to balance the small plane with letters and passengers, he tried to mask this inadequacy with exasperation.

'Can I just ask? This is the year 2000 where they tell me there are quite a few computers around. Why are we still doing sums with pencils and rulers?'

He was equally taken aback at dawn the next day when he discovered one of his passengers was a wildlife carer with a baby wallaby. He was obliged to take the little creature to the toilet when it became airsick and spent the rest of the journey trying to get rid of a bag of wallaby vomit.

Other challenges included nursing a baby crocodile, which he named Dickster, and chasing frogs out of the dunny for a frightened woman passenger. It was an original way to earn a living.

Bruce Gyngell, a breezy Australian, arrived from GMTV to take over as managing director from Paul Fox, and immediately informed Richard that he believed that 'presenters are the money'. Richard was a star in the early 90s due to *Countdown*; he should have his own company car and his own show. Accordingly, the title sequence for the pan regional (it was shown in Yorkshire and Tyne-Tees) *Richard Whiteley Show* had him climbing out of his large Jag. For one and a quarter hours every Sunday from October 1995 until the following February, Richard was ringmaster to a circus of bands, poets, ice skaters, collectors' corner and, especially, stars from Basil Brush to Dame Edna Everage. It was live and things went wrong – Edna's Rolls stalled because you can only have a trickle of petrol in a car in a studio for safety reasons – but this was part of the fun of the fair. Possibly, as John Willis reasoned, Gyngell did not quite have his finger on the pulse of the Yorkshire audience; Richard was more of a close friend than a distant star. The show was considered too expensive to do another series.

The BBC lured him away to do *Richard Whiteley Unbriefed*, a chat show in which he didn't necessarily know the star he was interviewing. This reached its apogee with Patsy Palmer of *EastEnders*. When I left the soap, Richard stopped watching so he had no idea who she was. Thus there took place a great unmeeting of minds. The public did not clamour for more programmes.

Much more successful was *Friday Whiteley*, where he could do his homework and thus deliver illuminating interviews with people as diverse as Alan Whicker and Claire Sweeney. It was very showbizzy and after the programme he would take the production team to Lee Chapman's club, Teatro, where they would party the night away.

As related earlier, Richard did not find success on *Celebrity Mastermind* due, not a little, to the fact that he set himself a ridiculously broad canvas – 60 years of the BBC – while others chose much smaller subjects. Nor did he distinguish himself in driving the Suzuki Liana in the BBC's *Top Gear*. Nigel Mansell was the winner in 1 min 44 secs, Carol Vorderman 1.51, Terry Wogan 2.04 and R. Whiteley 2.06 and last. To reach this incredibly slow time, he even managed to wear out two clutches and they had to wait for hours as a third car had to be found for him to break an all-time slow record for the show. He was even beaten by a blind driver. However, as I mentioned earlier, he triumphed in the BBC's *Hard Spell*.

They tried out a celebrity version of *Countdown* with such glittering names as Bamber Gascoigne, Magnus Magnusson, Ron Atkinson, Edwina Currie and Andy Gray, whose name is an anagram of 'Randy gay' – or is it the other way round? The programmes went out at 8.00 p.m. and, although good-humoured, this was not the right time slot for the faithful *Countdown* audience and the experiment was not repeated.

On the BBC *Mrs Merton* asked him if Richard and Carol had consummated their relationship yet and on Channel 4's *TFI Friday* he had his head chopped off and then went on a club crawl with Chris Evans, thereby enhancing his street cred with the young generation.

Both Richard and I were great fans of the Eurovision Song Contest. There was no question of us going out on the night that it was held; we were glued to the telly. I think the fact that it was brimming with joy and excitement and fun made it appeal to him.

In 1997 Katrina and the Waves won it for the UK with 'Love Shine a Light' so it was Britain's turn to host it the following year. (Katrina and the Waves sadly disbanded in

1999.) It was due to be held at the National Indoor Arena in Birmingham on 8 May and, to our delight, we were able to get four tickets from Terry Wogan's producer, Paul Walters.

Flushed with excitement, Dick rang Bob Warman to see if we could come and stay and communicated the great news that we had two extra tickets for him and Di. Bob said of course he would be delighted to house us, but he would rather chop off both his hands than go to the Contest. So we asked Peter and Christine Stewart and they were only too happy to join us.

There were 3,000 of us packed into the Arena for the three-hour show that would be seen in 36 countries. Paul Jackson, the producer, got us all singing Abba (winner 1974) songs to put us in the mood and it just swung along from there until Dana International of Israel emerged as winners.

Then the parties – every nationality, all over town. We bumped into Tim and Jo Rice and they got us into the BBC one where, for no apparent reason, people were dressed as bees – we later learnt these were accountants on a weekend course who, like us, had crashed the party. John Birt, the BBC Director-General, entered the room, looked shocked, and made for Peter Stewart who was dressed in a suit and looked like a television executive. We progressed to the Swallow Hotel which was full of American secret service men – Bill Clinton was due there the following day – and managed to penetrate the all-Irish bash where Terry Wogan was holding court.

There may have been more. All I can remember is emerging into a Midlands May dawn and Peter and Christine hailing a cab for their hotel which proved to be fifty yards away and Dick and I singing our way back to Bob's house in Edgbaston.

Because he used to joke about the name of a place in the Yorkshire Wolds called Wetwang, the less than two hundred villagers invited him to become their Mayor. Dick duly obliged and borrowed the mayoral robes of the mayor of Bradford for the photocall. From Mayor of Mafeking to Mayor of Wetwang, the Whiteley family had certainly spread its tentacles far and wide. Wetwang is an ancient settlement and its name is Norse, meaning 'rough coarse grass growing from a pool'. The village pond used to be graced by two exquisite black swans but one has sadly died.

Although Richard's early involvement with horses was not particularly distinguished, whether writing the wrong odds at ITN or failing to learn to ride with Graham Ironside, he loved to go racing – we both did – and invested in horses. His 'Arab' filly, Al Ava Consonant, seemed to enjoy admiring other horse's rear ends, so many did she put between her and the front of the field. When his trainer, James Bethell, came up with a promising two-year-old we named it Mare of Wetwang. 'One thing is certain,' he told the viewers when interviewed by John McCririck on Channel 4 Racing, 'she'll certainly run faster than the present Mayor of Wetwang.' And she won the first race at Ripon in September 2001 at odds of 14–1 (or 8–6 if Richard had been writing them, that being jockey David Allan's weight).

The Hon. James Bethell and his wife, Sally, were neighbours in Middleham – the centre of northern horse-training – and became great friends. James is a tall, elegant Harrovian with an accent to match but they have no airs or graces and loved a trip to the Coverbridge pub and a plate of egg and chips as much as we did.

There is a wonderful democracy about country life in the Dales with chums who are farmers, doctors, publicans, teachers, shopkeepers, builders and, in our case, the undertaker and his wife – Sandy and Debs. We had a life there that was little to do with the media but was, in essence, very simple and enjoyable because of good friends.

Not that Richard avoided people from work. Any party at The Parsonage would be full of them. And YTV even gave him a splendid dinner to celebrate his 60th birthday and retirement from the company in 2003. It took place in the magnificent dining room of Harewood House with its Chippendale furniture and portraits by Joshua Reynolds. Thirty of Richard's old colleagues were invited by the managing director, David Croft. Richard had always been a bit hurt that he never had a proper farewell from *Calendar* after serving 25 years but this did more than make amends. Judge James and I were included in the chosen few. David Croft sang his praise glowingly and when it came to Richard's turn to speak he did as he did at the *Countdown* Christmas lunches and went round the entire table with a customised tribute for every person there. Poor Austin had to wait until after midnight before he could deliver his speech.

On his actual 60th birthday on 28 December 2003, he gave a party at the Blue Lion at the bottom of our hill. This time friends and family were included. He pointed out to me a table containing two men talking to each other. One was Major General Charles Huxtable, the Commander of Britain's Ground Armies, and the other Norman Collier, the chirpy Yorkshire comedian. He was greatly amused to have brought them together, amused and rather proud.

I was happy, too. We had plans to expand The Parsonage, to buy a small flat in London and to spend more and more time in Portugal, which we loved.

But, as they say, if you want to make God laugh, tell him your plans.

SIXTEEN

The intensivist, Richard Davison, would take Christine and me into a side room and give us regular updates on Richard's condition. We used to call them 'terrible Tuesdays' because the bad news usually came on Tuesdays. Richard had developed endocarditis and would, eventually, have to have a new heart valve. There was the constant warning: 'He's not out of the woods yet'. That phrase came to haunt me.

He seemed always to be getting better – or was that just my wishful thinking? – with some days an improvement on others. He was able to get up and take walks round the room. I even brought in a television set so that he could watch *Calendar* to catch up on the latest Yorkshire news. This was a mistake. On 16 June it was reported on their news that various guest hosts had been lined up to present the programme while he was ill: Tim Rice, Lesley Garrett, Esther Rantzen, Barry Norman and Richard Digance. I knew of this. Tim had had the grace to telephone me and ask if I minded. Of course I realised that after an illness this serious Richard would take time to recuperate. But Richard didn't and the news upset him badly. I cursed *Calendar*.

Six weeks after he had been admitted to hospital, when most of his tubes had been removed, his breathing started to get more laboured and he was taken back into intensive care. The nurses teased him – 'We thought we'd seen the back of you' – and, laughing, he replied that he couldn't bear to stay away from them any longer.

The cardiologist had been regularly monitoring his heart. They didn't want to operate on him until the drugs had done their work and he had become much stronger.

I came in on the Thursday morning and, almost immediately, they asked my permission for him to have an angiogram. I turned to Christine and she explained it involved inserting a catheter into his blood vessel, injecting some dye to make the vessels visible and then taking X-ray pictures. I hated the thought of another invasive procedure but it had to be. I also agreed that Richard should be transferred to Leeds General Infirmary.

They didn't hang about. That evening I met Mr Prakash Kaul, the Leeds surgeon. He was friendly but frank. 'It's up to you,' he said. 'Unfortunately it looks from the angiogram that Richard has an abscess just where we want to replace the heart valve. It could end up being a twelve-hour operation but, in my opinion, if I don't operate he will die.'

He left me with little option, I felt, but to sign the form giving my consent. Richard was transferred to Leeds General and, by the next morning, was on the operating table. Mr Kaul rang me that afternoon. 'Better news,' he said, 'it wasn't an abscess, it was a rupture. We put in the new heart valve and sewed it up. It took less than five hours. It's gone very well.'

Christine and I were so elated that, after seeing a sleeping Richard, when we got to the Leeds waiting room we made phone calls to several anxious friends who had been in the dark as to what was happening and told them the good news.

By Sunday he was awake. Georgina and Tim came up from Cheltenham, to join me. We were, if not rejoicing, at least relieved.

We sat by him that afternoon. He still had a ventilator in so could not speak. Instead he squeezed my hand or touched my cheek or patted my hair.

'You realise you are in Leeds and they've fixed your heart,' I told him.

He nodded weakly.

The anaesthetist arrived and said it would be OK to remove the ventilator.

Richard had a fear of being left alone, so Georgie explained: 'We'll be back in ten minutes, Uncle Richard. They're just going to take the drain out.'

We joined the others in the waiting room to let the doctors get on with the job.

Shortly after four, a senior sister opened the door. 'I'm afraid we're having a few problems,' she said. 'His blood pressure has dropped. Mr Kaul is coming in.'

Evidently the rupture had burst and he had begun to bleed. There was no time to get an operating theatre prepared, so the surgeon would have to operate in the intensive care ward.

We were silent. I suspect we were all praying. Time froze. It could have been fifteen minutes or an hour and fifteen minutes before Mr Kaul came into the room.

There was no need for him to speak. 'I'm sorry. I thought I had saved his life,' he said.

Grief mixed with anger welled up inside me. I looked at Georgina. 'This cannot happen to this family again.'

After Richard had been tidied up, they let me go in to see him. He looked very tired. He had fought relentlessly against dying for nearly two months and now his nightmare was over.

Judge James came to pick me up from the hospital. On the car radio the news came that Richard Whiteley, aged 61, had died in hospital.

To say the next ten days were a blur would be an understatement. I returned to our home in Burley and my mother stayed the night and people filled up the house the next day. Not all of them friendly people – especially one woman journalist who invited herself into the kitchen.

Maggie shooed her out to join the gaggle of journalists and photographers outside. Georgina contacted Yorkshire Television who sent some security men over to keep the press further up the lane. I certainly had nothing to say.

The local coroner arrived. Somebody claiming to be Richard's sister had telephoned his office to ask if he had died of MRSA. Another press ruse: Richard's sister had been dead for seven years.

People phoned me, some of them heads of television companies and captains of industry, many of them in tears. I found it was me who was comforting them.

Iain came up from London in the late afternoon to stay with me in the house and help sort things out.

And in the evening Carol Vorderman arrived. She was utterly distraught. Richard's death had hit her harder then she could ever have envisaged, like the death of a brother. We just wept together.

In the house, we had been cocooned from the outside world but Carol had been at the Yorkshire Television Studios to record a tribute. She, too, had been inundated by the press, but this was her only interview.

She told us that not only had all of *Calendar* been devoted to a tribute to Richard but also half of the BBC rival programme, *Look North*, as well.

Terry Wogan had talked about Richard throughout his morning show and then Ken Bruce, too. There had been eulogies on radio and television news throughout the day.

The news had made all the front pages of the national papers.

'There's been nothing like it,' Carol said.

Iain opened a bottle of wine and we told stories about Dick. Carol recalled the time Richard referred to *Five Gays Named Moe* on the programme and they forgot to do a retake. She also remembered the day he came rushing into a meeting late because he had locked the keys in his Jaguar with the engine still running. He had been to call the AA, but Carol got hold of a wire coat-hanger and went out and prised the door open.

On Sunday, 26 June 2005 Geoff and Sue Druett had been due to fly to Spain. They had arranged a holiday in Catalonia with friends whom they met up with at Manchester Airport, only to learn that the flight had been cancelled. The airline put them up at the airport hotel where they ate early as their replacement flight was scheduled at four o'clock on Monday morning. Geoff turned off his mobile phone so that he could get at least half a night's sleep. When they got to the airport at the appointed time, it was announced that there would be a further long delay. Geoff, furious, switched on his mobile to berate the airline management. He noticed it was chock full of messages. Many messages but really just one message: sympathy that his friend and colleague had died.

He called me quite early to express his condolences and asked, in his usual modest way, if he could help with the funeral. 'It was what Richard wanted,' I replied.

Geoff postponed going to Spain, which enabled him to attend the inaugural dinner of the Yorkshire Centre Royal Television Society Awards at the Queen's Hotel in Leeds that Monday evening. It proved to be a sombre occasion, with everyone standing for one minute's silence in memory of Richard. David Lowen, the head of regional programmes and his boss, paid tribute to him. And when John Stapleton announced the award for the Best Presenter the name on the trophy was Richard Whiteley. But there was no one to collect it.

At the end of the evening it stood alone on a table on the podium. Geoff, without asking, removed it and brought it to me in our garden in Burley Woodhead the following day. He had shared a desk with Dick in the *Calendar* office and, because he was a religious man and a deacon of the church, Richard had said, a long time ago, that if he died, he would like Geoff to look after the funeral.

It was just about the hottest morning I can ever remember in North Yorkshire, airless with a temperature in the nineties.

Geoff, Iain and Georgie, with a couple of girls from YTV, sat round the garden table making funeral preparations. I found it hard to focus – three phones were going all the time – but managed to tell them Richard's favourite hymns: 'Love Divine All Loves Excelling' and 'Dear Lord and Father of Mankind'.

Iain had left the television in the living room on silent so that he could catch Wimbledon later. Judge James must have stopped to look as he came out to join us – just as his daughter, Georgie, was reading a tearful passage from Ecclesiastes.

'I wouldn't shag that Lindsay Davenport if she paid me,' pronounced the judge.

That certainly lightened the atmosphere.

When the others had left, Iain and I started to open mail, piles of it which the postman had brought. There were beautiful letters of condolence from friends in all walks of life, from Jean, our cleaning lady, and from Sarah, Duchess of York.

'Who's Gemma Grey?' he asked.

'Never heard of her,' I said. 'Maybe an old girlfriend.'

'I don't think so,' he smiled as he passed me the card.

Gemma lived in Hungerford.

It read: 'I can't believe how unbelievably sad I feel. I have never felt sad about the passing of a famous person other than the Queen Mother. The world will be a sadder place without him. Thoughts to Katherine and his family.'

It was the beginning of the most extraordinary phenomenon.

The next day Di, from the *Countdown* office, came round with a selection of pictures for me to choose one to go on the Order of Service at the funeral.

She also brought a sack of cards that had come to the programme and a hundred pages or more of email printouts.

'They keep coming,' she said. And they did. Somebody has subsequently counted that there were in total nearly a quarter of a million cards and phone calls, emails to the office and messages on condolences on websites.

It was not difficult to get in touch. The Post Office, when they had letters addressed to 'Richard – England' always delivered them to *Countdown*.

What Di didn't tell me, but I learnt later, was that on the Sunday night Richard died Lesley Garrett was already in the Queen's Hotel in Leeds ready to present the first five 'Guest

Countdowns' the next day, with the contestants housed in the Travel Lodge. Di was the first member of the team to learn that Richard had died and when she telephoned Damian and Michael there was no need to say that the recordings would be cancelled.

Richard's wish was to be buried locally with the cortege setting out from The Parsonage. Sandy, the Leyburn undertaker, was a friend. I laid out a familiar blue blazer with strong white stripes and a tie that had circles and squares in luminous shades of red and yellow and green and pink for Richard to wear. Later I pinned his OBE onto his lapel.

His funeral was held at 3.15 p.m. – the time *Countdown* would begin – on Wednesday, 6 July in St John the Evangelist Church, East Witton.

It was private – friends and family – but the church was full to overflowing. Bob and Carol and Geoff and Iain all spoke.

Bob referred to the many nice things that had been said about Richard in the media. 'One columnist wrote, "I didn't realise quite how much I liked Richard Whiteley until I heard the news of his death, and felt that a light had gone out in my life." '

Carol, his television wife, turned to the coffin and addressed him by her favourite titles:

'Richard Whiteley, the Mayor in the Chair, King of Countdonia, OBE.

'Richard often said that he was proud proud proud of being the first face on Channel 4 when he welcomed everyone to *Countdown* on Tuesday, 2nd November 1982. He was proud, and he had every right to be.

'Over the many years since that first day Richard was the man who millions of *Countdown*ers welcomed into their homes every afternoon without fail and who they came to love for the fact that he broke all presenting rules.

'They loved Richard because he wasn't slick but he was a cult. *Countdown*ers loved him because he wore jackets that could outdazzle Elton John and still think they were in good taste, because his ties were loud and his jokes were so bad they were "jokes only Richard could tell".

'When *Countdown* was extended to 45 minutes we became a show "of three halves"; instead of giving clues to the teatime teaser he'd muck it up and give the answers; he'd forget contestants' names and he could never understand a word that Scottish people said, which caused no end of problems.

'He would say ridiculous things, dig himself into verbal chasms and not know why we were laughing in the studio and it's for all of those reasons and many more that we grew to love him.

'All of our studio audiences came to see *him*, buses of students came from all over Britain with their Richard Whiteley T-shirts and bad ties they'd borrowed from their dads. Students would roll about in the audience laughing, everyone wanted his autograph and a photo with him. He revelled in it and they all went home happy.

'Beyond the walls of this church and through his parlour game, many people came to smile with Richard. This last week, *Countdown*ers from across the world have expressed their thoughts for Kathryn, for James and for Richard's family.

'We estimate, because we have not been able to count them yet but we will, that *Countdown*ers have sent more than 250,000 messages and tributes. Here's one:'

From Helen Hooper in Barnet, London.

You were my afternoon comfort blanket. You were my sit-down between work and getting the supper ready. You were my friend, but I never met you. Goodbye and thank you Richard.

'Richard,' Carol went on, 'You never could resist reading a final letter from a viewer even when Cindy and Damian were shouting in your earpiece for you to stop. So here's a bit of banter fodder written by Ray Cornell from Saffron Walden, who sent this message to an Internet website last week when your last recorded shows were being shown, and it says it all.'

I know that Richard would want me to watch the end of the series, and laugh at his unfunny but funny jokes and I have tried.

I've tried very hard. I would like to make a nine-letter word and get the numbers right every time and solve the conundrum, but there must be something wrong with my television screen ... I can't see the picture clearly any more.

The last to speak was Iain. He ended with kind words for Christine and for me.

'Kathy understood Richard better than any other woman, except perhaps for Helen, and these last eight years have been of increasing contentment and harmony and devotion for both of them. She made him laugh and she cared for him with a fierce passion.

'Especially in these last two months when he was ill and she stayed by his bed in intensive care, giving him hope every day that he would fully recover.

'Two other women were rocks, not just throughout this period but during the harrowing deaths of Helen and Alex: Helen's sister-in-law, Christine Stewart – the Florence Nightingale of North Yorkshire – and Helen's surviving daughter, Georgie, who has not only shown unbelievable courage in the face of these tragedies but taken control of the situation in a time of grief.

'In the spring of next year, Georgie will marry Tim at The Parsonage. It is Kathy's intention to remain there, so she can be near Richard's grave.

'And when Kathryn dies, she will be buried beside him. So they will be together. Again.

'When Georgie telephoned me to say he had died, I thought I had lost the brother I never had. But, in these intervening days, I realised I had been privileged to have had, for 40 years, the friendship of the nicest man in the world.

'Good night, Dick.'

A small party of us – family, Bob and Di, Iain and Mo and their daughter, Sophie – followed the coffin to the plot I had chosen for him in the corner of the churchyard. The rolling Yorkshire countryside stretched for miles in front of us, with low skies, solemn and grey. A soft rain swept across the churchyard. Maybe the Dales were weeping.

So there his body lies. If he were able to, he could look up the hill and see The Parsonage.

SEVENTEEN

As James drove me home after saying goodbye to Richard for the last time, the news of his death was already on the radio. It was an affectionate tribute but I did not want to hear it and, from then, until long after his funeral, I avoided reading newspapers or listening to the radio or watching television.

Even now, more than a year later, it is not very easy to look at the reactions which some very kind researchers, Michelle and Alexander, put together for me.

Sadly and suitably on the night he died, it led the *News at Ten* on ITN, where Richard had begun his broadcasting career. He would have been proud.

'Richard Whiteley, the much-loved presenter of Channel 4's *Countdown*, has died. He was 61 and suffering from pneumonia. He had a long and distinguished career. He started his career as a local reporter but it was *Countdown* which made him a household name. He presented every edition for 23 years.'

ITN devoted the first three minutes of their national news to their former employee, with images of him at work and receiving his OBE from the Queen and some very emotional tributes. Nick Owen, their Royal Correspondent and a friend of Dick's, told viewers that he was a very genuine man. 'A lot of people in television are not, in real life, what they seem on the screen, but Richard was. He had a long and distinguished career in television. I remember him telling me he was going to do this local quiz programme for a few weeks. He didn't think it would last – neither, in fact, did I. But he went on to become the first face on Channel 4. The programme worked solely because of Richard. I'm devastated.'

When Richard died, Georgie had first telephoned Iain with the news and then Carol. Carol realised that she was likely to be inundated with calls that night so, before she took her phone off the hook, she told her agent, John Miles, who publicly confirmed Richard's death.

'Carol Vorderman, who co-presented *Countdown*, was said to be distraught. Her agent John Miles said, "Carol is absolutely devastated. He was such a good friend whom she loved dearly. They had 23 years of making programmes together – that's about 4,000 programmes. He was very special to Carol. She heard the news of his death at 8 p.m. It is all the more difficult because of the shock. As far as we knew he was making good progress. It was hoped that at the end of the summer he would be back making *Countdown* programmes again. Carol is having great difficulty in coming to terms with what has happened."'

Alex Hall, a friend of Richard and mine, traditionally hosted a phone-in on Radio Leeds at eleven on a Sunday night. She, too, was distressed: 'It's always sad to have to report the death of someone and this death has particular sadness to me. Richard Whiteley, I'm afraid, has died this evening leaving, no doubt, many people completely lost without him. He was a lovely man who I have worked with on many occasions and socialised with and I'm sure many people are very, very shocked by the news. I'm sure he will be deeply mourned by Kathryn, his partner.

'I saw him last, I think, at last year's Great Yorkshire Show and people would come up to him and he just got on with everybody. He was great, a great character one of the most significant characters we've ever had, I think, in Yorkshire and I for one personally will miss him very much.

Alex's phone-in that night was due to be on the subject of 'Do Manners Matter?' but there was only one subject that Yorkshire people wanted to talk about on 26 June 2005.

Betty rang in from Bridlington. 'What a shock, Alex. Somehow we expect these lovely people to go on forever. Wetwang will be in mourning tonight.'

Brenda, from Sheffield, told Alex about her evening: 'I came upstairs to get my things ready for work in the morning and my husband just came to the bottom of the stairs to tell me he's dead. It's like John Peel. You feel poleaxed don't you? It sounds dramatic and he's not family but you feel poleaxed because he came into your lounge. He came across as genuine.'

Helen, from York: 'I can't believe it. It's awful – it's really, really awful it's like losing a friend, isn't it? I would just like to express our really, really sincere sympathy to all his family and to his partner Kathryn Apanowicz. He was a lovely, lovely man and he will be terribly missed. We are praying for him and Kathryn.'

Even a former dinner date phoned in: 'I remember going with him to what is now my favourite restaurant. He took me there for the very first time and he was a bit of a tinker – don't speak ill of the dead. They had a special menu on that was a bit cheaper before 7.30 and we got there just on 7.30 and he persuaded them – bless him, he just charmed them into giving it to us at the earlier price.'

And, finally, Phillip, from Leeds: 'We met him in a restaurant. He was so nice and kind. My wife doesn't like his programme and she told him that – your terrible jackets, you need training in taste, you need a makeover.' And he just laughed and he said, 'Oh, well, that's your loss,' and he was really good about it. He was such a nice personality. My wife is in tears at the moment.'

One person who was unaware that Richard had died was Mark Witty who had produced him in *Calendar* and many of the off-shoot programmes, like *Friday Whiteley* and *The Richard Whiteley Show*. He had gone with his father to the regular Sunday night pub quiz at the Coach and Horses in Harrogate. The first question in every quiz was the same: 'Have you turned off your mobile phones?' Mark had, as usual, turned his on to 'vibrate' and had noticed an unusual number of vibrations for a Sunday evening. He was due to produce *Calendar* the following day and began to suspect there must have been a breaking Yorkshire story that he needed to put a reporter on immediately – maybe a pile-up of returning weekenders on the A1 or possibly a fishing trawler missing.

He made for the men's room and into one of the cubicles, locking the door. To his surprise there were no less than eight messages. He decided to begin with the one from Will Venters, YTV's head of news. His boss answered immediately.

'Will, what is it?' asked Mark.

'Haven't you heard?' came the solemn reply.

Will was already in the newsroom and Mark, having made sure his dad could get a lift home with a friend, was there within the hour. To their credit, neither man believed that this could possibly happen. They were so certain that Dick would walk out of Leeds General Infirmary. So they set about from scratch compiling the story of Richard's life and his 37 years working for the company. After a few hours' snatched sleep, a slimmed-down version was played into the early morning GMTV programme. Duncan Wood, a former GMTV reporter, now doing Dick's old job on *Calendar*, would present it.

The BBC were quicker off the mark as Christa Ackroyd, Richard's former co-presenter who had been head-hunted by the BBC's *Look North,* was told the news.

'Anne Monks from *Countdown* rang me on that Sunday evening and she just said, "He's died" and I said, "Well, he can't have done." Because, while he didn't seem to be getting any better in Bradford Royal Infirmary, the thought when he went to Leeds was that he was on the up and was starting to move.

'I was stunned. I went back into the living room and said to my husband, "Richard's died." I had to retreat into a room by myself and just be on my own. Then, within the hour, I was getting calls from *News 24, Breakfast TV*, radio stations asking me to come on – and newspapers. It just dawned on me that this was huge.

'I don't think Richard would have known that everybody was very quickly latching onto the personality that he was and thinking it was a momentous news story. He would never have predicted, and neither did I, that in all the papers in the morning he was front-page news. I thought: "God, he is really famous. England's most famous Yorkshireman."

'The next day everybody said, "I am so sorry to hear about Richard," because they knew how I would be, even in the street. When I went to pick the milk up, they said, "You must be really upset. I am so sorry to hear about Richard."'

The following day he was indeed front-page news in every paper. Not 'Ferret Man Dies', as he had always predicted. Not even his own preferred alternatives of 'Perceptive TV Interviewer Dies' or 'Cuddly Afternoon TV Host Dies'.

Instead there were photos of him everywhere, with captions such as the one in the *Mirror* – 'Modest. Loveable. Charming.' Followed by the headline: 'TRIBUTES POUR IN FOR TV'S *COUNTDOWN* KING'.

The *Guardian* wrote: 'Deceptively bumbling, he used an acute, Cambridge University-trained mind to establish an exceptional place in the country's affections. Had Yorkshire ever voted for independence, he would have been chosen president of the new republic by a landslide.'

'One of the best-known and most popular faces on British television,' said the *Daily Telegraph*.

His local paper in Burley, the *Ilkley Gazette*, reported that the Yorkshire flag would fly at half mast over Burley for the week; it was usually only flown on Yorkshire Day. The editorial read: 'To say that the late Richard Whiteley was larger than life is something of an understatement. He was a man for whom the phrase "needs no introduction" could have been coined. With his infamous collection of outlandish jackets and ties, allied to an engaging and mischievous personality that was both delightful and infectious, he was almost a national institution.'

The *Yorkshire Post* bestowed the title of 'Mr Yorkshire' on him. 'He was the kind of man who gave everything he had to make the best of what was good in his life. No false front, no fake modesty, no affected self-promotion. Such men are rare as rubies – and here was one of them.'

And so on and so on. To list any more would be lacking in modesty but Richard would have been pleased to learn he had become 'iconic'.

There was widespread reaction on radio and television that Monday morning with Lorraine Kelly and Philip Schofield on *This Morning* talking about Richard's death, and sending me their best wishes – and Terry Wogan, Ken Bruce, Jeremy Vine and their listeners all expressing their sorrow in their separate ways.

The bosses at BBC Leeds, realising how saddened Christa must be, told her to stay at home. But she didn't. 'I went into the BBC at ten o'clock. I said I had to be in, I wanted to cut the obit for lunchtime.

'At first, I didn't want to read it and then I thought, "Well, no, I will read the lunchtime" and I cut it and I read it. I trawled the archives and watched a hundred pictures in our studios, pulled the archives up from the BBC, got permission from *Calendar* and sat myself in an edit suite. I have never done an obit on a friend before. Do you know, though, I never ever shed a tear. It was so important that it was right. It had to be, as Richard would say, a performance and if you think that sounds cold, it's not cold.

'And then I went straight back into the edit suite, we did longer in the evening. What other news mattered? Him dying was all everybody was talking about. They didn't say "Richard Whiteley dying", they said "*Richard* dying".

'We did 15 minutes – the first half – then we did the rest of the news of the day. At the close we said, "Let's recap: we have lost a friend" and we ended with a picture of him in our studio, laughing. I walked out of the studio and I went into the Green Room and I sobbed and sobbed and sobbed. But I had done the performance, I had done the programme. It was everything I had learnt from him.'

Over at his native *Calendar*, Will and Mark had no doubt what their viewers expected. They devoted the entire half-hour programme to Richard with no mention of any other news. His greatly loved niece, Georgie, her father, his brother-in-law, Judge James, Anne Monks and Carol were all interviewed.

Georgie told the viewers: 'When he was in Bradford Royal Infirmary he received hundreds of get well wishes every day – cards and letters from people of every age and from all over the country. He had prayers written for him by people, poems and the odd pun. So some people wrote, "We're counting down until you get better" and lovely things like that which did bring him great cheer. And Kathy read them to him every single morning. They started off with him having a pigeonhole at the BRI and in the end they ended up giving him his own post room!'

And Carol could barely restrain the tears. 'Of course he was coming back – he was coming back to us and we thought perhaps he would be back to do the summer programmes and then we realised that probably he wouldn't be and we consoled ourselves that Dick would be back in September. *Countdown* is a family. It's been all of us together for all of these years and Kathryn too, and Richard was very special, a very special person and over the years I've worked with lots of different people and as I often told him – there's only one Richard Whiteley. He made us cry with laughter every day we were in studio and you rolled your eyes at these terrible jokes that only Richard could tell, and as the years went on he got happier and happier. He would burst into the studio. He was such a happy man.

'*Countdown* is now nearly 23 years old and often in recent years, we would have whole studio audiences that were younger than *Countdown* itself and he would revel in it and the girls would have Richard Whiteley T-shirts printed up with his photo on, and he would love that and he would love signing them particularly and the boys would raid their dad's wardrobe and pick their dad's worst jackets and ties and there would be rows of them who had all brushed their hair like Richard over on one side and he thought that was hysterically funny and they loved him. I calculated it this morning, because I knew Richard would want me to, that about a quarter of a million people have been in our studio audience over the years and they all fell in love with him.'

Among the prominent people who had taken the time to pay tribute was our friend and neighbour William Hague, the former Tory leader. 'Whenever you walked into a function or a room and Richard was there – you thought, well, now I am going to have a good time – I needn't have any worries about this being a boring event 'cos Richard Whiteley is here and we're going to have a good laugh and that was what you could absolutely rely on with him.'

He had known another prominent politician, David Mellor, for much of his life. 'We were both at Christ's College, Cambridge. There was a paradox about Richard – on the one hand he tried to pretend he was just a lucky guy and yet he was a very able man – very insightful, very clever, very thoughtful about politics. Above all, someone said to me last night – a few of his friends were ringing round – when you think of Richard, you smile. We just had so many laughs together. He was just a great guy to know. He would regularly come to our house and this will sound stupid but Richard would transform any party – I remember we had a very good dinner, quite a lot of wine drunk and we put on an Abba record and everyone there was forced by Richard to sing 'Thank You for the Music' and you had to get it absolutely right. We probably spent an hour rehearsing and it sounds daft but he made it one of the greatest hours of my life. Last summer I was sitting in a hotel in Capri and suddenly this stomach comes around the corner closely followed by Richard Whiteley. He was on a boat with another famous Yorkshire businessman, and so on Capri, and even people who didn't have a clue as to what these stupid English people were on about were completely captivated. That was Richard – he could take over your life.'

That was the summer Dick and I went on holiday with Lord and Lady Kirkham on their yacht.

Duncan ended that edition of *Calendar* with the simple but true observation: 'Richard loved Yorkshire and Yorkshire loved Richard.'

And there the public tributes might have ended but a strange thing happened. They went on. There was something in the atmosphere that journalists had an instinct about.

The next day both *The Times* and the *Guardian* did exactly the same thing. They put another picture of Richard on the front page and then devoted the entire cover of their supplements, *T2* and *G2*, to him – a photograph of Richard when young for *The Times* and with Carol in the *Guardian*.

A former contestant, Andy Bodle, wrote:

'Whenever people find out I was on *Countdown*, their first question is always uncannily predictable: "So what's Richard Whiteley really like?" So much so that my response, over the years, has become parrot-like: "I know he comes across as a bit of a knob, but he's actually a lovely bloke."

'When I went to Leeds to compete on *Countdown* 12 years ago, a nervy youth of 23, I fully expected to be stuck in a room until I was due on set, then ignored by the cast and shouted at by the production staff. In the event, while certain members of the cast swanned in two minutes before recording and swanned out again afterwards, Whiteley made a heroic effort to put the contestants at ease. He chatted to us in the green room beforehand; on set, between takes; and especially in the bar afterwards. He did two things that most celebrities never do: he asked questions, and he made a grand job of feigning interest in the answers.

'He also dispelled another of my illusions. I'd always supposed that TV was scripted from first to last, that speaking out of turn was punishable by death. This did not apply to Whiteley. [A fact that did not endear him to the show's producers; if you ever wondered why his expression sometimes became strained, it's because his headset was filling up with words that Carol could never have put up on the board.] If the on-set banter seemed as if it was made up on the spot, that's because, more often than not, it was.

'He had his flaws, of course. Rumours have always wafted around, for example, about Whiteley's eye for the ladies. And it's true that, when my glamorous mother came to support me in the Champion of Champions two years later, he did spend slightly too long grilling her on the finer points of racing. But his flirting, according to Mum, was more candid than conniving; and, being rubbish, impossible to take offence at.

'You can't even blame him for the dreadful puns. The howlers that littered Whiteley's opening spiel every day were the producers' work. In fact, when said producers discovered that I was a budding scriptwriter, they insisted that I write his links for the next two shows. And you know what? Having my jokes read out by Richard Whiteley was a prouder moment for me than winning the bloody series.'

One of the minor consolations to come out of Richard's death was that a number of good causes were able to benefit. These ranged from the touching to the funny. We held an auction of just a few of his infamous blazers and ties in September, which raised £850 for Macmillan Cancer Relief. There was also a Richard Whiteley scholarship established, which began in October and gave a talented youngster £11,000 a year to cover the cost of the tuition, accommodation and equipment, as well as, hopefully, a couple of glasses of wine in Richard's memory – always a prerequisite for a young journalist!

Lucy Mangan wrote the main piece in the *Guardian*. She started out by saying how her sister used to hate Richard but in the past years had begun to appreciate him.

'Whiteley, with his odd attire, old-fashioned mien and avuncular air, started to become something of a refuge from encroaching blandness in television. He became a rare beast, a television personality untainted by the desperate, clawing need for fame and consequently the beneficiary of an inchoate affection that was part nostalgia for a time when imperfections and idiosyncracies were tolerated rather than airbrushed and Autocued away, part simple hunger for authenticity and part admiration for an almost heroic indifference to change and to fame. He resisted reinvention so we did it for him. And then, as my sister so eloquently put it, he went and died.

'Bugger.'

EIGHTEEN

E very Saturday morning I get up at 6.00 a.m. and drive across the Dales and over the Hambleton Hills to York to do my radio programme. In the winter it is a dark and sometimes dangerous journey if snow has fallen in the night and the roads are not yet sanded. But in the summer it lifts the spirits. I put down the roof of the car and smell the hedgerows; posses of racehorses with their stable boys and girls make their way to the gallops and the undulating fields are dotted with lambs, white and perfect in the dawn sun.

Such days help me get into the breezy mood that, I hope, carries along my three-hour programme for Radio York. It is a combination of interviews with anyone from gardening experts to visiting authors, phone-ins, quizzes and some repartee with Doug in the radio car who is frequently at a fair or village event. All this is interspersed with my favourite music or, sometimes, purposely chosen music. If you need to go to the loo during a live show the secret is to put on a record like 'American Pie' which lasts more than eight minutes!

On Bank Holiday weekends Richard would usually do the show with me. He had a prolific knowledge of Yorkshire and sometimes revealed it in the form of a quiz. What are the opening words of what has been described as Yorkshire's National Anthem and are sung to the hymn tune 'Cranbrook'? 'On Ilkla Moor Baht 'at'. Why does St Peter's School in York never have a guy on its bonfire? Because Guy Fawkes was an old boy. Is it true that Yorkshire has more acres than there are letters in the Bible? Apparently so. Somebody set themselves this task and calculated that there were 3,906,940 acres in Yorkshire but only 3,566,840 letters in the Bible.

When Richard was a child, one of his heroes was the broadcaster and Yorkshireman, Wilfred Pickles, whose *Have a Go* quiz on the radio got more than 20 million listeners. Richard always wanted to revive it with me as 'Mabel at the table' giving them the money. But it was not to be.

We would sometimes stay in York after the show and explore The Shambles – a series of narrow, twisting medieval lanes which are mentioned in the Domesday Book – or sometimes we visited York Minster, a magnificent edifice which was first built in 627 and now charges a fiver to get in.

But there was no charge on the afternoon of Thursday, 10 November 2005 when a Memorial Service for Richard was held there. I was apprehensive about this. I had wanted a service in Giggleswick chapel; cathedrals are for monarchs and prime ministers, not daytime game show hosts. But the people at YTV had assured me this should be the place. And they were right. The cathedral was packed to overflowing: nearly 2,500 people. And the streets outside busy with onlookers and media with York's town crier John Redpath, in his flame-red jacket and tri-corn hat, ringing his brass bell outside the Minster as the crowds made their way in, calling out, 'No amount of words on a scroll could say how the people of Yorkshire feel today.' His sentiments were greeted, I was told, with warm, spontaneous applause.

Geoff Druett, who once more had headed up the team organising the service, suggested to Richard's YTV work mates that they might like to meet for lunch beforehand. 150

turned up. 'He would have been thrilled and flattered at the turnout of old colleagues,' Geoff said. 'These people have not been seen together in one place for decades.'

The newspapers were interested in the well-known faces among the arriving congregation: Jo Brand, Alan Whicker, Austin Mitchell, Lesley Garrett, Barry Cryer, Derek Wilton from *Coronation Street*, Gyles Brandreth, Richard Stilgoe, Sir Bernard Ingham (Baroness Thatcher's former press secretary), and of course Carol.

Some of them stopped for the TV cameras. Alan Whicker said: 'Mention his name, and people laugh, which is nice. He led his life in a nice happy way, and he was a man with no enemies as far as I'm concerned. He was a prince.'

Lesley Garrett confessed: 'Every time I think of him, I smile. He's sorely missed. A happy face, wonderful ties – a great bloke.'

I wanted this service to be a celebration of Richard's life and work. I didn't want it to be a sad event, but a cheerful tribute and a happy memory.

I started proceedings off by talking about how this was a memorial for Richard or Ricco, Ricardo, Dickie or Dick. I usually called him Dick. Richard was the name I reserved for when he was in the doghouse. I referred to the fact that he used to claim he had two wives – myself and his 'TV wife', Carol – but also that women had been important to him his entire life, from his mother Margaret and sister Helen to his nieces Alex and Georgina. Sadly, Helen and Alex had 'left the party too early', as he used to say, but Georgina was able to give a tribute to a man who was more than just funny puns and silly jackets.

Georgie was most moving. 'During the days following Uncle Richard's death, I found myself in bewilderment, listening to tributes on the *Today* programme and reading long obituaries in the papers and watching footage of his friends on the television,' she said. 'I realised that, up until his death, I had never appreciated how famous my uncle really was. At home in Wensleydale with Kathryn, Richard was in his element. He was fond of nesting, pottering, making his home warm and welcoming. Having a glass of chilled Chardonnay always on hand for unexpected visitors. He treasured time spent with people that he loved, surrounded by possessions and memories that provided comfort and continuity with the past. For me, Uncle Richard was not the man of the garish jackets and the luminous ties, but of the navy jumper and comfy shoes. Bringing in coal from outside. Lighting the fire. Making tea and enjoying family jokes.

'Even from a young age, Richard had the ability to make people laugh and feel at ease. His infectious smile and chuckle could elevate even the lowest of spirits as many viewers of *Countdown* have so kindly expressed in their letters to the family. When Richard walked into a room, you were aware of a quick wit, a sharp intelligence and a warmth, decency and sensitivity. There was a deeper side to Richard that expressed his compassion for those in need and his spirituality, which encompassed not only his faith but also his respect for and delight in society's great traditions and institutions.

'His love of family was another reason for staying so close to his roots. He adored in particular his sister, my mother Helen, whom he would speak with most days, after *Coronation Street*. The squabbling of childhood and teenage years gave way to a close friendship and a deep loyalty. When Helen died just over seven years ago, Richard was devastated. He missed her deeply and thought of her every day. Richard hated illness, both when it affected him and others. I believe this was heightened by the prolonged illness of his niece, my sister, who struggled so bravely with cystic fibrosis up until her death just two years ago. Richard felt her loss with a deep pain. He had hated to see her suffering and was appalled at the way illness had conditioned the way she had to live her life.

'In his own words, Richard said he had had a marvellous time. He did, tragically, leave the party too early. I would, though, like to give thanks before God for Richard's life. For his passion and his wit and his sensitivity and his love. He is irreplaceable, inimitable. The void that he leaves is formless and vast. And yet, as long as we have words and images and thoughts of Richard in our minds, he shall never truly die.'

Dear Georgie. Not even the premature deaths of her mother, her sister and, now, her uncle, caused her to question her faith.

We had hymns – Richard's favourites such as 'Love Divine, All Loves Excelling', 'My Song is Love Unknown' and 'Jerusalem' – but also his favourite songs: Gershwin's 'Someone to Watch Over Me' and 'I Got Rhythm' In his heart, Richard wanted to be a song and dance man. However, his dancing would always include him sticking his fingers out and putting his tongue out, making him look energetically ridiculous. His singing also left a great deal to be desired. While the rest of us were trying to sing in the key of B, so did Richard – B flat. As I have written, there was a certain song which summed up being the last to leave a bar, and it was Sinatra's 'One For My Baby and One More for the Road'. It was beautifully sung by David Owen-Lewis.

Carol told the congregation that Rick Wakeman, once of Yes, once a *Countdown* fan and then a Dictionary Corner guest had, one evening, played a very beautiful song on the piano, entitled 'Gone but Not Forgotten'. Richard was very moved and said: 'Will you play that for me when I go, old boy?' So Rick did – at York Minster.

Sir Paul Fox, the former Managing Director of Yorkshire TV, paid a professional tribute from one journalist to another:

'Up in the celestial television newsroom, our friend Richard is still reading the obituaries that filled the newspapers on 27 June. The affection and the warmth were glowing comments, and underlined the high regard so many had for Richard. Richard had an old-fashioned view of the world. He believed in traditional values. He was a man of the people. There was nothing high-handed about him. Too often he was too modest about his achievements.

'He was a founder member of that talented team of young journalists who devised and launched the nightly news programme, *Calendar*. It soon became compulsory viewing. Over the years, Richard became its anchor and its conscience. The programme meant everything to him. Richard was with *Calendar* for 27 years. His colleagues will confirm that he always stayed true to his profession. With *Countdown*, what began as a pilot six episodes turned into a run of nearly 4,000 shows over 23 years. There isn't a programme I can think of with such a lifespan. While the game was its strength, Richard gave it zest, humour and humanity. We shall always remember him, not just in our heads but most of all in our hearts.'

Carol Vorderman spoke of her fond memories of Richard:

'The last public event that Richard and I went to was in April this year, before he fell ill. We went to present a prize at the British Book Awards in London and there was this lovely lady sitting next to me and Richard leant over and said, "Delighted to meet you. I absolutely love your books." Anyway, this lady was then ushered away to present an award and I turned to him and said, "Gosh, you are well-read aren't you, Whiters?" and he said, "Oh yes, I love that Joanna Trollope." I said, "No, Richard, that was the actress Patricia Hodge." And then, as only Whiteley could, he made it worse by sending her a bunch of flowers the next day saying, "I'm sorry, I thought you were a trollop."

'He was the best company you could possibly wish for. When you were with him, every time you were with him, you laughed. Whiters would have loved today. His audience, choristers and dignitaries and household names. And everybody here for one reason, to talk about him. Because of Richard, *Countdown* remained one of the most important shows on Channel 4 for 23 years.

'In all of that time, *Countdown* never won a single award. For years, we trudged along to the National Television Awards at the Albert Hall and we knew we'd lost before the awards began, because we were plonked in what we call losers' corner. We would sit there and we would practise our 'losers' faces for the cameras. Richard would get hysterical, laughing. He would always say: "Remember our motto, Vorders, we never win," and he'd laugh. And we never did win.

'And, Whiters, if I could speak to you now, all that award-losing flashed by too quickly. I just wish we could have lost together for many more years than we did.'

His chum, Gyles Brandreth, was there to tease him.

'For once, I think the tabloids may have got it right. Richard was indeed a love god. Women adored him. They were right to do so. He was very loveable and very funny. I remember him taking me into his dressing room at Yorkshire Television. It was, of course, immediately adjacent to Carol's dressing room. It had been newly decorated. But Richard had discovered a strategically placed hole in the partition wall. He told me that, initially, he was going to report the hole to security. And then he thought, "To hell with it, let her look." '

Another chum from Dictionary Corner was Barry Cryer, a Yorkshireman like himself. And, like Gyles, a humorist and wit:

'Richard was great fun away from *Countdown*. When you were out with him at what was loosely described as lunch, it was more like a one-day match when bad light never stopped play. He was a joy to be with as he was always interested in other people. I was out on the loose with him more than once in Edinburgh during the Fringe and the young ones would shout out: "Lord Whiteley!" And he would ask them to come over.'

The Dean of York said prayers and we sang 'Jerusalem'. Then it was off to have a drink and talk some more about the man I loved. The man we all loved.

On the back of the order of service there was a short poem:

Teatime will never be the same
Without Wetwang's Mayor to play the game;
For it can be said, indeed quite rightly.
They'll never replace old Twice Nightly.
His gentle fun with the awful pun
And the taste in ties never outdone.
But the Countdown's *run and now it seems*
The angels will share his Gypsy Creams
So thank you, Richard, for a life that merits
A place where you'll find only friendly ferrets.

Of course I miss him. Always look on the bright side and all that. The problem is – he was the bright side. Barry Cryer once produced a brilliant poem on *Countdown* and Richard made him promise he'd do another one. That day, in York Minster, he kept his promise.

Now is the winter of our discontent
10 letters, 3 vowels, but it was meant
In another context by the Bard.
In this setting, it is hard
To come to terms with the inescapable fact
That we are missing the top of the bill act
Uncle Richard – he was never Dick
Neither was he ever clever Dick.
But our chum, our mate, our pal
Avuncular (9 letters) and I shall
Always remember our Mr Bumble
Our beadle – not you, Jeremy – ever humble,
Almost arrogant in his humility
Because he saw his role to be
The servant of contestants, not their boss
No wonder that we feel the loss
Of that smile, those glasses, those jackets
Was the hanger still in there? I look back, it's
So recently we spoke and it's now clear
That we rejoice, because our host is here.
And, furthermore, I have a hunch
Somewhere he's having a marathon lunch.
But I'll be run out of town upon a barrel
If, at this juncture, I do not mention Carol.
They were as one, a four-legged joy,
The Dream Team – Buttons and the Principal Boy.
But now I close and though 'tis alien
To me use words that are sesquipedalian
14 letters (many-syllabled) I must, I do
As a final toast to Richard, who
Was my friend, a man for all reasons
A practising catalyst in all seasons,
I'm celebrating Richard, I'm no mourner
So now I retire to my Dictionary Corner,
My words run out, I am struck dumb
De de

De de
De
De
De
Dum.

APPENDIX

After Richard's death, there was a flood of individual tributes. I had expected people to write and say something about how they felt, but nobody could have been prepared for the size and sincerity of the reaction that we had. It seemed as if everyone who had ever seen Richard on TV, or had read about him in the press, wanted to say something. Even the papers, which had been so kind and generous about him, seemed surprised at the scale of what people had to say.

The *Countdown* office was frozen. The YTV switchboard could not cope with the calls and it became impossible for the *Countdown* staff to find their mail since it was somewhere among the tens of thousands of cards and letters that were brought in sacks to the office. Every paper that had written about Richard received letters, phone calls and emails.

A lot of people took the trouble to write personally to me. All of their comments were particularly touching and thoughtful. Many of them were couples, often pensioners, who had been watching *Countdown* since, in some cases, its first-ever episode. Many people had also lost someone in the past, and were able to empathise on that level.

Kay McClaren of Waterlooville, wrote to me and to the *Countdown* team:

> I have to let you all know how very saddened and shocked we all feel about Richard's passing. He was an important person to us and made many a bad day bearable. I wish there was something I could say or do to help you all.

On a similar note, Chris Woodrow wrote in to say that it would have been her husband's birthday on 27 June, and, like some others, enclosed a poem that affected her:

> *You were the other half of me, a heart linked to my own,*
> *What do I do with half a life, now I am on my own?*

It was also kind of her to mention the times when I had been on the show, as she said that it 'let us get a small glance at your life together'.

Margaret Allen, in addition to sending me a beautiful hand-made card, said how deeply sad she was by the loss, and how 'half of me wants *Countdown* to continue, and the other half wonders how it will other than as a lasting tribute to a lovely man'.

One writer, Doreen, was kind enough to make a donation in Richard's memory to the local children's charity 'Bluebell Wood Appeal'.

Kathie and Alex Simpson, of Sherborne, wrote about how they spent their afternoons 'laughing at the jokes about Richard's jackets, ties and wigs', and how they welcomed the fact that 'he took them in his stride, and always had a comeback'.

Nor did former contestants forget Richard. I had a long card from Jack & Sheila Male, in which they told me about their grandson Gary, and how he had got onto the finals. As a result of his appearance, he was offered a job by a firm in

Spain, which he became manager of, and that he had got his brother a position there as well. The card went on to say that these were wonderful results, all due to Richard. 'I have no doubt in saying that Gary would have been one of dozens that Richard helped, because he was full of compassion regarding his contestants, it showed on his lovely face, who we will dearly miss seeing, but he will never be forgotten.'

Joyce Forrest said: 'To me it was like losing one of my family, someone who visited me in my home every weekday'. Similarly Josephine Hurry wrote:

Everyday, he came into our homes, and was like a dear friend who knew when to leave. I will pray for him, as I do for my family, and I will pray for you and Richard's family. I wish he hadn't left so early.

John & Liz, like many others, said:

Words cannot express the loss of Richard. He was such a lovely, funny 'natural' man, it must have been a joy to work with him. His jokes left a lot to be desired, but *he* always enjoyed them. If someone should have asked me who I would like to go to dinner with, it would have been Richard Whiteley. A total gentleman.

A few kind people mentioned that they were sorry for me, or for Carol, but it was affection for him that dominated. Mrs Betty Hill wrote: 'We are saying prayers for you all at this very sad time . . . Richard was to us, as to many people, one of the family.'

Josie and Rohan Sagar pointed out:

There was more quality in Richard than stars in his eyes . . . he appeared unspoilt by his fame, kind and heart-warming, not what you would normally expect of someone who turned out to have such star quality! Things just won't be the same.

Nearly everyone referred to *Countdown*, and how much watching him on afternoon television had meant to them. People said how much they liked him, despite not, in most cases, ever having met him. 'I felt I knew him,' was how they explained it.

Neil from Abingdon wrote about how he used to watch the programme with his mum, and that she passed away a few years ago, but Richard's presence always gave him happy memories of her. The Morgan family of North Yorkshire wrote a particularly touching tribute; they lived in a village close to The Parsonage, and often saw Richard doing his weekly shopping. Their younger children called him 'Uncle Richard', and their daughter always kissed him goodbye through the TV screen at the end of every show.

All kinds of people wrote in; the only thing they had in common was their love and respect for Richard. An Oxford English graduate, Sophie Gregory, told of how she and her friend, Alex, used to fool their tutor, Dr Atherton, into thinking that Richard was a very distinguished professor of Chaucer and Old English and kept quoting him in their essays. Knowing Richard's love of literature and books, they knew that he would have approved. Their ruse came to an end when, having used Richard as a critic in one of their essays, the tutor became very interested in reading his scholarly texts – which were sadly non-existent.

Many students and student unions wrote with their condolences, saying that he was a cult figure in their common rooms, and that he'd distracted many from their lectures and essays at half past four. The *Independent* published Richard reminiscing about his fame as a student icon:

After appearing at Leeds University, he recalled: 'The girl students were fighting to try on my glasses and give me a drink of their beer. Then they'd shriek, "Oh, he's drunk from my glass!" The president of the students' union said, "We've had a few pop groups in here, but I've never seen anything like it!" '

On 29 June 2005, Richard's great friend and former *Calendar* colleague, Austin Mitchell, made a tribute to him in the House of Commons, submitting an Early Day Motion.

'That this House is saddened by the sudden death of Richard Whiteley, OBE, Mayor of Wetwang and Yorkshire's best-loved television personality, the first face to appear on both Yorkshire Television and Channel 4, presenter of *Calendar* for 25 years and *Countdown* for 23 and, as a proud Yorkshireman, the nicest man on TV as well as one of the funniest, a man known round the world for his kindness to ferrets and other interviewees, and the biggest customer of the ludicrous jacket producers of Bradford, notes that Richard leaves 528 ties, 186 jackets, a host of sad friends and a world less colourful for the passing of his five vowels and 11 consonants; and bids him "Ave atque Vale" (Hail and Farewell) as they say in Harrogate.'

The BBC even opened a website where people could email their tributes.

Like everyone else I was very saddened to hear of Richard Whiteley's death. He was a truly natural television performer whose apparent bumbling style endeared him to viewers across all age ranges. I have many happy memories of watching *Countdown* from the very first night of Channel 4's existence. The love and respect he and Carol Vorderman had for each other was obvious on screen and was one of the show's many strengths, and my sincere sympathies go to Carol as well as Richard's family. I do hope Channel 4 will be brave enough to continue with *Countdown* – I am sure Richard will relish the chance to watch it himself for a change.

Simon, Gosport, Hampshire

I can't believe how unbelievably sad I feel. I have never felt sad about the passing of a famous person other than the Queen Mother. The world will be a sadder place without him. Thoughts to Katherine and his family.

Gemma Grey, Hungerford

Richard was loved by so many people and will be fondly remembered for his ties, humour and cheerful manner. Our sincere condolences to Katherine, his family and the *Countdown* team. He will be sadly missed.

Lily Bartle/John Underhill, Chepstow

My hubby and I have watched *Countdown* for years and our afternoon teatime will now never be the same again. How we will miss the jokes only Richard could tell, the jackets, the ties, the magic of the interplay with Carol and the guests in Dictionary Corner. My heart goes out to Carol in the loss of her special friend, and especially to Kathryn in the grievous and untimely loss of the love of her life. I really enjoyed it when Kathryn was a guest in the Corner: it was obvious that she loved him to bits and that they sparked each other off as a couple, so different yet so ideally suited. Gosh, I am sad and will miss him as much as any dear friend, but my feelings are as nothing compared to Kathryn and Carol. God bless you both in these coming days. Thinking of you.

Margaret Addie, Kelso, Scotland

I can't believe that Richard Whiteley is no longer with us. I remember watching him on the first episode of *Countdown* and on many more along the years. He never had an edge – always pleasant and courteous and with a wicked sense of humour. Our screens will be a sadder and less joyful place without him. My thoughts and prayers are with Katherine and his colleagues at *Countdown* – especially Carol.

Beverley Price, Nupend, Glos.

The death of this truly lovely man – a gentleman, will leave such a gap in so many people's lives. He gave us all so much enjoyment. Heaven will be a brighter place with Richard and his ties!

Josie Dyson, Shirrell Heath, Hants

I remember watching *Countdown* on the day Channel 4 started, and I watched it every afternoon when I got home from school with my Mum. It was a good show because of the game itself but a great one because of Richard Whiteley and those truly awful jokes. I still catch it when I can and will miss his humour and humanity. My Mum passed away a few years ago but the publicity around Richard's death has brought back very happy memories.

Neil, Abingdon

I went to a recording of *Countdown* two years ago and I met Richard. Such a warm-hearted gentleman. He will be sadly missed. And I will miss seeing him twice daily on television! For I watched the morning show as well as the teatime show. Goodbye, Richard.

Wendy Parker, Lincoln

Have there ever been more tributes from 'ordinary' people following the death of a celebrity? I think that says it all about how much Richard was loved, and what a genuinely nice person he was.

Ian, Edinburgh

Finally, Christa Ackroyd said goodbye to Richard in the *Sunday Express*:

Oh, how he would have loved this week: every newspaper, every headline, tributes from all four corners of the globe, TV programmes, even the Yorkshire flag flying half-mast in his home town. What really hurts, though, is that Richard Whiteley, who would have chuckled and puffed out his ample chest with pride, wasn't here to know how much people thought of him.

He could never have imagined a tribute in Parliament, a statement from the Queen that she was saddened to hear the news and the scores of people who queued to sign books of condolence or register their sympathy on the Internet that for years had completely baffled him.

But then that was the measure of the man. He never really understood how he had got to where he was, never accepted that he was an icon, a national institution and as far removed as possible from the throw-away TV celebs that are here today, gone tomorrow.

I want to tell you about the Richard Whiteley behind the TV persona of stripy jackets and appalling ties – but there was no other Richard Whiteley than the one you saw day in and day out. Ask him to describe the phenomenon that became *Countdown* and he'd tell you that it was just a simple little parlour game. Ask him how he'd be remembered and he'd trot out the same line that his obituary would read: 'Ferret man dies.' But then who could forget that wonderful moment when the ferret handler told Richard, ferret dangling from his finger, to put her down, that she would not hurt him and Richard replied: 'But she *is* hurting.'

Despite the fact that his face was among the best-loved on our screens, with 10,000 appearances to his name, his naïvety and approach to life, that was on occasion almost child-like, were the very essence of the man and his charm.

The only time I thought Richard had succumbed to the fame game was at his 60th birthday, when a huge, white Bentley with RW1 was parked outside the pub where the celebration was to be held. 'Richard,' I said, 'Have you treated yourself?'

'Not at all,' he answered, and out stepped the instantly recognisable Rick Wakeman.

He was so endearingly eccentric that I've laughed until I've cried at his stories and his sense of *joie de vivre*. I once attended a school speech day at his beloved Giggles-wick to find that Tricky Dicky, as we lovingly knew him, was somewhat less tricky that day than he had planned. Slightly worse for wear after a late night, he had grabbed the first pair of trousers to hand to go with his regulation blazer and old school tie. If anybody noticed that they bore the wide satin stripe of a dress suit, they didn't tell him. Why would they? He was a ray of sunshine, a true eccentric, who laughed at himself more than anyone else.

Every afternoon in the YTV green room, Richard could be found watching that day's episode of *Countdown*. Not because he was vain but because he thoroughly enjoyed it.

He'd laugh at his own jokes and try to work out the word game that he had himself presided over. It was that laughter that was so infectious and will be so hard to replace.

Less than two years ago, on his 60th birthday, he said there would never really be a place for a TV star like him in today's self-obsessed, body-perfect culture. He also said he was the luckiest man alive. No, Richard, we were the lucky ones to have known and loved you.

1943–2005

INDEX

KA denotes Kathryn Apanowicz, RW denotes Richard Whiteley.

ACKNOWLEDGEMENTS

Books do not write themselves and I certainly did not write this book by myself.

There was Jonty Sale who covered the crimes and misdemeanours of Richard's time at Giggleswick and Cambridge, and Graham Ironside who helped chronicle his exploits on *Calendar*. Thanks to all the friends and family who were interviewed and lovely Joe Eaves who typed them all up, as she did for Dick. Natalie Jerome of Virgin is a publisher of rare discernment and Ben Mason, still in his twenties, an agent destined for greatness. Iain Johnstone not only helped me put this book together but also helped me put my life back together, and his daughter, Holly, by transferring Dick's duties to me, made me Britain's first female godfather.

Kathryn Apanowicz
The Parsonage
September 2006